W9-ABP-749

Plow Naked

Poets on Poetry **Donald Hall, General Editor**

DONALD HALL	*Goatfoot Milktongue Twinbird*
GALWAY KINNELL	*Walking Down the Stairs*
WILLIAM STAFFORD	*Writing the Australian Crawl*
DONALD DAVIE	*Trying to Explain*
MAXINE KUMIN	*To Make a Prairie*
DIANE WAKOSKI	*Toward a New Poetry*
ROBERT BLY	*Talking All Morning*
RICHARD KOSTELANETZ	*The Old Poetries and the New*
LOUIS SIMPSON	*A Company of Poets*
PHILIP LEVINE	*Don't Ask*
JOHN HAINES	*Living Off the Country*
MARGE PIERCY	*Parti-Colored Blocks for a Quilt*
DONALD HALL	*The Weather for Poetry*
JAMES WRIGHT	*Collected Prose*
ALICIA OSTRIKER	*Writing Like a Woman*
JOHN LOGAN	*A Ballet for the Ear*
HAYDEN CARRUTH	*Effluences from the Sacred Caves*
ROBERT HAYDEN	*Collected Prose*
JOHN FREDERICK NIMS	*A Local Habitation*
ANNE SEXTON	*No Evil Star*
CHARLES SIMIC	*The Uncertain Certainty*
LOUIS SIMPSON	*The Character of the Poet*
WILLIAM STAFFORD	*You Must Revise Your Life*
TESS GALLAGHER	*A Concert of Tenses*
WELDON KEES	*Reviews and Essays, 1936–55*
DONALD HALL	*Poetry and Ambition*
CHARLES WRIGHT	*Halflife*
WILLIAM MATTHEWS	*Curiosities*
CHARLES SIMIC	*Wonderful Words, Silent Truth*
TOM CLARK	*The Poetry Beat*
WILLIAM MEREDITH	*Poems Are Hard to Read*
PETER DAVISON	*One of the Dangerous Trades*
AMY CLAMPITT	*Predecessors, Et Cetera*
JANE MILLER	*Working Time*
DAVID LEHMAN	*The Line Forms Here*
HAYDEN CARRUTH	*Suicides and Jazzers*
DANIEL HOFFMAN	*Words to Create a World*
GREGORY ORR	*Richer Entanglements*
FRED CHAPPELL	*Plow Naked*

Fred Chappell

Plow Naked

SELECTED WRITINGS ON POETRY

Ann Arbor

THE UNIVERSITY OF MICHIGAN PRESS

Published in the United States of America by
The University of Michigan Press
Manufactured in the United States of America

1996 1995 1994 1993 4 3 2 1

Library of Congress Cataloging-in-Publication Data

Chappell, Fred, 1936–
Plow naked : selected writings on poetry / Fred Chappell.
p. cm.—(Poets on poetry)
Includes bibliographical references.
ISBN 0-472-09542-0 (alk. paper).—ISBN 0-472-06542-4 (pbk. : alk. paper)
1. Chappell, Fred, 1936– —Aesthetics. 2. Poetry. I. Title.
II. Series.
PS3553.H298Z47 1993
809.1—dc20 93-23791
CIP

A CIP catalogue record for this book is available from the British Library.

For Mary Jarrell

Contents

Introduction

All the writing about poetry that I am guilty of has been in complicity with those who asked me to do it. As a poet and fiction writer, I do not find much impulse toward formal criticism in my temperament. But I have usually obliged those who invited me because of vanity or economic consideration, and so I will not try to evade responsibility. The opinions collected in this volume, however cranky and ill informed, are the best reactions I knew how to have.

Some of them I no longer entirely agree with. Not having an ideological agenda in regard to poetry, I have not been able to hold to abstract fixed standards. Probably I would not care to do so anyhow; each separate work of art implies its own aesthetic principles and I take the discovery and elucidation of these to be part of the job of a receptive reader. What I say about one poet in one place may be contradicted by different responses suggested by a different poet. I am not proud of my inconsistencies, but regard them merely as data. The inconsistencies may say something about me as a person, but my first task was to say something heartfelt about the subject at hand.

Though I may have formulated no settled philosophy of poetry, I do have prejudices of which I am rather proud and I have not tried to hide or to excuse them. I am in favor of poetry; I regard it as an inescapable quality and product of human physiology and an important element of all human society. Such cultural importance lays a heavy responsibility upon the poet; his duties, it seems to me, are as well defined and socially important as those of the soldier, the policeman, and the schoolteacher. He may not always succeed in fulfilling these duties, but he should always be aware of them.

And the poet should also take note that such duties are going to take some toll of personal life, just as they do of the lives of other public servants. For one thing, the poet will be ill paid, just as the soldier is and the sewage plant worker and the fireman. One of the ways to know how useful your job is in American society is to look at your salary; if it is low, your job is probably important to local well being.

So that criticism of poetry sets hard standards upon the critic; insofar as poetry is a public material, the critic's purpose is to keep in mind the possible consequences to society of the poetry that he reads and to form some part of his judgments in this light. I believe that the best poetry—that is, the lines with the best use of language, that most honestly engage the poet's feelings and intellect—has the best possible social consequence. The immediate political or religious or ethical cast of a poem is of secondary importance in estimating the possible good of the lines in regard to society. It must be first a truly good poem before it can be truly good for much else.

That is what the critic tries to judge—and now we can all speak in chorus: "Well, he's certainly got his nerve!"

Yes he does indeed; I can attest that a critic has more foolhardiness than is good for any organism. It is not that he fears he might be wrong in his pronouncements; the truth is that he knows for a fact that he will be found wrong as time goes on. We might formulate it almost as a scientific theorem: the mistakeness of a poetry critic's judgments increases in direct proportion to the amount of time that elapses after he has made them. Criticism has a way of looking natty, smart, and sometimes even profound when fresh in print, but the years are rarely kind to it. It may fall into its palsied dotage in only a few weeks.

I do not much care about this hazard because even where I have imagined poets or poems to be at fault, I was always on their side. Poems, being produced by human beings, will have faults that proceed from a common humanity. What makes poets uncommon and most often draws my admiration is their readiness to express their thought and to show the extent of their mastery in such an exposed way. They are willing to look completely foolish in order to say what they feel they must say. When they fail—as most of us are bound to do—the fact is not widely remarked, but the poet always knows, and knows that in that moment he stands alone.

In one of the pieces included herein, a phrase from Vergil turns up. *Ara nudus, sere nudus.* Plow naked, sow naked. That, I think, comes close to defining the poet's task. The words are rather too grand to apply to the critic's task, but they do help to keep it in focus. The poet's field grows up luxuriant if he is a good plowman, and the critic is there to help tend the garden—circumspectly to suggest weeding and pruning, but most of all to admire, to praise, to fetch the watering can.

First Attempts

The real beginning of a writer's compulsion to compose is difficult to discover and he must be a foolhardy author who will attempt to sound these strange, moiling, storm-lit depths in search of an origin. The first time he sets words on paper he has already forgotten why he ever desired to do so. The job before him, finding the best arrangement of the words his subject matter demands, is so taxing that his concentration must focus there—outside himself—and the vague longings and shapeless wishes and half-remembered regrets and dusky fears that brought him to this decision are sealed away, perhaps forever. The first serious pass a writer makes at a page changes his interior life so drastically he can never return to his incomplete earlier state of being.

He has been forced to be objective about something, to try to see it in a light that permits description, however fumbling and inaccurate. Even if this something is only his own subjective feeling, he has made the first step backward necessary to focus upon it. He has divided himself; he has learned that *to feel* and *to see* are not identical activities but complementary ones. If he continues to write he will understand that seeing is more important than feeling and that his emotion must be guided by what he is able to understand of his subject. This stage of development is analogous to that earliest breakthrough a percussionist makes, access to the complementary independence of different parts of

From *My Poor Elephant,* ed. Eve Shelnutt (Atlanta: Longstreet Press, 1992).

his body, the ability to play separate rhythms with each of his hands and feet.

It is not so complicated or unnatural as we might like to make out. After all, this division of our faculties is one we all must resort to when we try to make important rational decisions about matters with which we are emotionally involved. We step back; we try to take account of our feelings and to see how they may be affecting our judgments. This division of faculties is not habitual with us, but it is hardly uncommon. For the writer, though, it must become habitual.

A more dangerous phase of development comes shortly afterward. There arise now two conflicting impulses: the need to write, and the desire to be a writer. The beginning writer—let us put his age at thirteen or fifteen or eighteen years—can hardly articulate and certainly cannot visualize the need to write. But *being a writer:* that is easy to imagine.

At least it was for me at age thirteen. And fourteen. Fifteen. Sixteen. I knew what I would look like as a writer. During my working day, I would wear a tan cotton shirt and trousers of vaguely Australian cut and sandals with broad thongs—because of course I would be living in a tropical climate. That was my working outfit. I would own a great many other costumes, being an enormously successful novelist. My wardrobe would include cowboy outfits, detective trench coats, suave tuxedos, spotless laboratory tunics, and all the rest; these would be the togs in which I gathered the raw materials for my writing.

I knew too what I was supposed to look like while writing. I was to sit in a director's chair before a steel-topped table and squint at the keyboard of my ancient and trusty Royal through a picturesque swirl of Chesterfield smoke. Without removing the cigarette, I would hammer out sentence after telling sentence, paragraph upon paragraph of breath-stopping excitement. For revision, of course, another atmosphere would be required. (Oh yes, I already knew that a writer revises.) To revise—no, to *polish* the morning's work I would dress in tweeds and sit outdoors. During this process I would smoke a briar pipe and sip brandy. But I would be ruthless. The blunt red pencil in my tanned athletic fingers would tear through the awkward phrases and unnecessary adverbs like broadsword strokes; the new constructions would be written in beautiful tiny black calligraphy with Waterman's finest point. This draft of the manuscript would go to my private secretary for final typing. The salient points of this sexy girl changed from time to time, as I learned to appreciate a variety of females, but the worshipful gaze she cast upon my manuscripts remained constant through all my daydreams.

But then the daydreams changed. I began to fancy that I had become serious about poetry; I was reading Shelley and Shakespeare by wholesale acreage and had bought a copy of Yeats's early plays for twenty-five cents from a junk dealer. As a poet I would have no leggy adoring secretary. (Alas.) No wealth, no public acclaim. I would live lonely in a neat little cabin on the edge of Pisgah Forest. I would study the religions and sciences and philosophies, each in its original tongue. I would *commune with nature.* Wisely, sweetly, I would write long poems by the light of a kerosene lamp. My death would be little noticed and my poems unregarded for half a century. Then they would be discovered by a scholar; the critics would be astounded, the reading public grateful; my name would be carved on the lintels of libraries.

That was a heady sensation—to have lived happily but obscurely, to have died solitary and unappreciated, to have received at last my just acclaim, and, best of all, still to be alive at age fifteen.

I suspect that most writers are urged to their purpose by adolescent fantasies such as these, and that these daydreams do not entirely evaporate with adolescence. In even the most seasoned scribbler there probably arises a pale green tender shoot of hope each time a new book is in the works. He doesn't dare think the thoughts fully, but the echo of his early glossy reveries rings faintly in his head. "This is the one, the one that breaks through to the green clover field of paradise where swarms of readers mass to my books like bees to lonesome blossoms." The steely frost of publication soon lays this pastel hope a-withering but never kills it entirely.

Even so, and even in his youngest years, the watchful writer tries not to indulge too freely in these fantasies. Already he feels that such daydreaming is antagonistic to his goal. Something has caught his attention—the look of a hillside in the moonlight, the white hands of a jeweler, an aunt's swollen ankle bulging painfully over the strap of her shoe, a locust fencepost patched with lichen and crooked with weather, its rusty staples loose in the grain—and he wants to express what he sees and feels. He knows for a certainty—without knowing how he knows—that if he can fix the image of that fencepost clearly and suggestively, if he can cosset it with his language until it replies in its own secret speech, he shall have accomplished something worth doing, a step necessary in the development of his powers. He knows too that the image of himself as a writer of popular bestsellers or as a forlorn hermit stands between him and his fencepost and that he must wipe away his wish as if it were breath-mist on a cool window pane in order to see the true lineaments of his desire.

The person who wants only to be a writer, who has no larger hope or finer design, may well become a writer and may well become no more than that. But the person who actually wants to write is almost guaranteed a more savorable existence than the other, if he will pursue faithfully the disciplines of the art. A religious person may find comfort in the Gospels and strength in prayer, but the person who puts himself through a regimen of spiritual exercises will possess a deeper life, happier and more tragic, even though it may not be his temporal life that he seeks to improve.

Yeats's poem, "The Choice," is well loved, but my experience discovers its dichotomy a falsity:

> The intellect of man is forced to choose
> Perfection of the life, or of the work,
> And if it take the second must refuse
> A heavenly mansion, raging in the dark.

For me it is in the work that the final perfection of a life is lodged; the work is the life. One of the grand things about writing is that it never stops; the writer is not always sitting at his desk, but he is always writing. This fact marks too one of the most wearying things about the discipline, that there is no escape from it. The writer is sentenced to a lifetime of observation, of analysis, of emotional rigors; he is sentenced to a lifetime of sentences.

Perhaps when I come to be as wise as Yeats I shall agree with his poem, shall acknowledge that the intensity of focus demanded by writing debilitates one's natural charity. But I have not seen such attrition to happen. I have known any number of writers who were drunks, buffoons, knaves, clods, blowhards, sycophants, trimmers, charlatans, and egomaniacs; indeed, I can find episodes of my own life in which I have matched each of these descriptions and sometimes all of them together. But I cannot hold my writing to blame for my character faults and in fact I believe these would be profounder if I did not write. I believe this of other writers too; insufferable as they are, if they did not write they would be worse, they would be justifiably exterminable.

Not that writers as a group are scurvier than other groups. Maybe it is a holdover from my adolescent glamorizing that I expect them to be better than other people, more considerate, self-effacing, decisive, brave, strong, loyal, trustworthy and on their honor to do their best as Boy Scouts. I entertained the notion that the worthiest of vocations draws the worthiest of people—and then betters them. But it doesn't seem to work that way.

When I was a teenager the only contemporary writer whose personal life I knew anything about was Hemingway. *Life* magazine was always running photos of the animals he had slaughtered, the bottles he had downed, the movie stars he had companioned. He possessed exactly everything a writer was required to possess: global fame, wealth, athletic prowess, important friends, expensive gear, and a beard.

It didn't take long, though, for my fantasies to reject this future; the image was too rich for my palate and even as a teenager I suspected that the Hemingway of the photo journals was an unreal phantasm conjured up by press agents. His was a heady way of life but not for me; I foresaw that I would have responsibilities that I would betray if I tried to live like Papa. ("Papa" was what Marlene Dietrich called him, according to *Life,* and I knew deep in my soul that no movie star was ever going to call me Papa.)

What these responsibilities would be I could not say. It is characteristic of some writers to feel the brunt of their responsibilities before they have been able to imagine the kind of writing they must produce in order to give rise to these duties. Somehow or other they hear the first throbbings of the tone they will be required to strike and then they begin to meander unsteadily toward that distant sound. I knew that I was not going to make a sound like Hemingway; I knew that the glamorized image of Hemingway stood between me and my fencepost.

But if not him, then who? The only other writer of whose personal life one ever heard anything was Poe—and he was regarded as both scandalous and tragic. Whenever my parents, teachers, and ministers tried to dissuade me from a life of writing—as they did regularly and assiduously—it was the fate of Poe they threatened me with. They pictured him as a wild-eyed genius who was an alcoholic and drug addict, and they hinted too at darker vices and nearly incomprehensible sins.

Well, I could see that being Edgar Allan Poe had it all over being Ernest Hemingway, but Poe belonged to history. The past was irrelevant; I felt that no one in that fusty demesne ever encountered problems that shared any kinship with my problems. The model I was looking for had to be someone in a situation like my own who had overcome the same complex of drawbacks to become globally acclaimed or fairly successful or even just a writer who had published something, damn it all to hell and sideways.

The trouble was that I on my side and my well meant, minutely benevolent antagonists on theirs made too much of my ambition to write. To all of us it seemed such an exotic occupation, such a dangerous ambition, that when we tried to imagine the way of life a writer might trace we could come up with only the most lurid and improbable scenarios, visions that horrified and repulsed my elders while they attracted me with all the force a two-ton electromagnet exerts on a single crumb of iron filing.

If I'd been bright enough to look around me, I would have seen that my little drama was being enacted in the homes of many if not most of my friends. Our part of the world offered little opportunity for careers. If the good times kept rolling a young man might take his father's place in the paper mill—that kind of arrangement actually obtained—but he would have to wait for his father to retire. If his family owned a farm he could starve on his own hilly property. The usual jobs in selling, clerking, building, accounting, and so forth, were soon filled up. So the boys decided to head out to Detroit or Pontiac or Flint; there were little Appalachias in those towns, whole settlements of "briars," as we were called in the factory cities, and maybe they could find a toehold in the tenements. Others headed for the military; mountain boys were especially attracted to the Air Force where they imagined themselves set down in the Elysian Fields of engine-tinkering. A lucky few were able to go to college. But in order to find careers, to make their lives, they had to leave their families and strike out into the unknowable world, and regret and disappointment, sorrow and anger accompanied their leave-takings of their tight-knit mountain families.

What I didn't say was: "Well, look at Joey Swain. He's going into the Army where he's got at least a chance of getting killed. I don't see how trying to be a writer can be any more dangerous than that." If I'd had sense enough to see the world around me in these terms then my parents and the other friendly dissuaders might have been able to do the same. But none of us did, and the conflict continued and became less amicable as my high school years began to come to an end.

I think I understand now a little better this one particular source of the conflict. They too had once enjoyed fancies about undertaking careers of the kind I proposed, and had rejected these ideas out of prudence. Perhaps they too had been advised by their parents that the stuff of dreams was not bankable, that the road that looked to lead to stardom actually led to starvation. Perhaps they felt that their present security in the world had been founded upon their early refusals to follow their desires.

I got an inkling of this possibility on the eve of my departure to Duke University. My father and I walked up the hill to her house so that I could say goodbye to my grandmother. She had attended Weaver College and recalled it pleasantly. My mother had attended Carson-Newman College and then had transferred to the University of Tennessee. This evening my grandmother mentioned that some of my mother's "things from college" were still stored in that closet there in her parlor. I rummaged and, sure enough, found textbooks, annuals, photographs, some letters and buttons and dance cards, and a school newspaper in which I discovered a poem signed Ann Mae Davis. When I showed it to my father he at once devised a practical joke that seemed as tame as a butterfly. "Copy it down on a piece of paper," he said. "We'll tell your mother it's something new you've written. I'll bet a pretty she won't recognize it."

She did, though. As soon as I read the first line her face flushed scarlet and grew puffy and her eyes filled with tears. She rose from the table crying *No* and left the room with little choppy heartsickening steps. My father and I looked at one another ashamed. We had blundered terribly but we weren't sure how. It is obvious to me now that my mother had harbored literary aspirations and that the fond misery she had made of my adolescence (with a lot of help from her son) was in part an outcome of these thwarted desires.

She would not have been alone in her hopes. The desire to be a writer is a common one, after all—as common as the desire to write is rare. Among her friends and acquaintances there must have been other ladies and gentlemen with literary ambitions. Some measure of literary learning has traditionally been part of a southerner's make-up, and an Appalachian, not thinking of himself as southern exactly, is likely to look to the southerner as a model of cultivation. So here was another reason why she and her peers felt they had authority to try to turn me aside from literature: in their minds they had tested the possibility for themselves and found it lacking in substance. Or maybe they found it frightening. Usually the most daunting thing to people who want to be writers is the prospect of having to put words on a page, one word and then another and another, spelled more or less correctly and punctuated more or less logically.

When she came back into the room and resumed her chair at the supper table she had recovered pretty well. The subject of her writing was not taken up again at that time or ever again in her mortal years. The memory of the expression on her face when she tottered out remained vivid in my mind, and in my father's too, I expect.

But she must have suspected something when my father asked me to read from my work. They never asked me to do that; they didn't want to hear what I wrote, they didn't even want to hear about it. My bedroom was too small to accommodate a desk and typewriter, but I had found a niche in the upstairs hall. When I set the Royal clattering the sound could be heard all over the house. Visitors who asked about the racket were informed that Oh, that's only Fred working on his typing. Their embarrassment was just that acute; I was not trying to write, I was learning to type. Typing was a useful skill that might come in handy someday. Writing was impractical, and impracticality was worse than heresy, thievery, or some kinds of homicide. These were the tag-end years of the Depression; it was imperative to be practical.

I'm making my parents sound like obtuse Victorian parents, like the parents of Beatrix Potter, say. They were not; they were sweet and decent people in difficult economic circumstances who were stuck with a wayward child. They indulged me in all sorts of whims and vagaries, some of them rather expensive, as when I decided that I might be taking an interest in photography or chemistry. Probably they hoped that in these passing fancies some fascination might arise that would supplant my determination to write. In the life of most families there comes a time when the offspring begin to assert their need for independence. As often as not the child fixes upon the one matter which represents independence in his mind and which his parents cannot abide. "Anything but this," they say. "We want you to be happy; you're free to do whatever you want to do. Except become a rock musician—or an artist—or a hang glider—or homosexual—or a soldier of fortune—or—" But for the young person, it is *this*, this one thing and no other, upon which his future appears to depend.

Some quality of self-pity always tincts a writer's memoirs as it does the memories of most other people who consider themselves successful in some degree. Those who look upon their lives as having failed are sometimes able to point to imperfections of their characters or to elements of their circumstances as being the causes of ruin, and they may examine these facts in a sort of complacent wonderment. But the successful person likes to picture himself as advancing triumphant over the obstacles that hindered his way; he likes to find a legendary outline in his career. He forgets those who aided him in ways hugely important at one time but which seem less important as his self-satisfaction overcomes his sense of history.

In my case, a lot of people were willing to aid. I could write substantial tributes to Tom Covington, Lynn Hickman, my high school Latin teacher Mrs. Kellet, and to a few other high school teachers who knew of my ambition to write and found it, if not laudable, then at least harmless and fairly amusing. I have tried to write a lengthy essay about my beautiful friend at Duke, Dr. William Blackburn, and have twice failed. I wrote a sketchy tribute to Reynolds Price, but have never paid proper thanks to Hiram Haydn, James Applewhite, George Garrett, Peter Taylor, and others. The list of my literary creditors is impressive both in its size and in the prestige of its names and it lengthens year by year. I owe more to scores of my students than I can ever say, however much I want to say it.

But most of these friends belonged to the future. Now I sat in the upstairs hall facing the tongue-and-groove pine paneling and clack-clack-clacked at pages of what I thought was fiction, what I hoped was poetry. It was stifling up there. Drops of sweat slid down my sides from my armpits; my hair matted, and I breathed with my mouth open. In wintertime, though, it was freezing, and I had to keep flexing my fingers and blowing on them.

I wrote mostly fantasies, ghost stories or horror stories or Arabian flights or science fiction—a great deal of the latter. It was not that I had no realistic experience to write about; there was God's grand plenty of realism on a farm. But I found it impossible to organize experience into any kind of shape; reality may have had the advantage of authenticity but it had the disadvantage of stubbornness, of sheer perversity. It didn't want to be whittled, rearranged, or even comprehended; it just wanted to sit laconic in an ungainly lump and refuse to differentiate into parts. The Canton High School library contained two books about writing, both with short chapters on fiction which set a lot of store by plotting. Plotting real experiences proved impossible; plotting what I made up proved to be fairly easy—a little too easy. So my stories were flimsy little contraptions with unexpected, often unexpectable, endings. The characters were colorless except for some single livid trait I laid upon them like the impress of a branding iron. The setting of any story was as insubstantial as a soap bubble, the characters' motives as murky as the vagaries of our foreign policy architects. Style was—. . . .

But there is no reason to go on in this vein, denigrating the literary efforts of a hapless adolescent whose writing may be, for all that I can tell, not so much worse than mine is nowadays. It was not important that the writing be good; however good or bad it was, I would be forced to move away from it as my majority came on. The important thing about the writing was that it got onto the page. Wanting to be a writer was not standing in the way of my searching for words and patching together clauses, misplacing phrases and dangling modifiers, overusing dashes and whirling on as capricious with pronoun references as a March breeze with a girl's rayon skirt.

I learned to write more or less in the same manner that I learned to type: by doing it so dreadfully wrong that now and then I would hit upon something acceptable by merest accident. Then I had to recognize what made my discovery useful, to try to repeat it and to build upon it. This was a process as painful as adolescence itself, but in my case just as necessary. My way of learning to write presaged the method I would pursue in learning anything else; an eon of trial was followed by an infinitude of error. I didn't fret, though. I knew that the climb was going to be long and steep; in fact, it was *supposed* to be. Writing was not something anyone could just pick up and perform perfectly from the start; it was different in that respect from ballet or skiing. Writing was a product of blood and toil, sweat and tears. I had invested enough of each of these, I thought, to insure my eventual success. Even if I failed, I was vindicated. In order for someone marvelous to succeed, someone like Henry James, say, whose *The Turn of the Screw* had become one of my favorite novels, then perhaps someone like me had to fail. And in cooler moments I recollected that I hadn't really shed any blood—my parents had only boxed me about a little—and had shed no tears either.

Because rejection was no great sorrow. I sent my stories off to *The Saturday Evening Post,* to *Story,* to *Astounding Science Fiction,* and, most frequently, to *Weird Tales,* and they were promptly returned to me with form rejections on little blue slips. I was not disheartened, but a little jealous when I heard that Tennessee Williams had sold his first story to *Weird Tales* when he was only seventeen years old, and when I saw a photograph in a fashion magazine of Truman Capote lying petulantly on a sofa and looking to be about fourteen. Science fiction was an especially daunting genre in this regard because so many of its famous practitioners—Isaac Asimov, C. M. Kornbluth, James Blish, and a lurid squadron of others—had begun to publish and to establish enviable reputations in their teenage years. It was true that in the 1930s there was much less competition in the field, and true too that one never found in the anthologies the earlier efforts of these authors, but they had accomplished the first main thing a young writer feels that he must accomplish: they had published professionally.

Before I went off to college I published only a very small amount in the professional magazines. I am not going to talk about that because by the time it happened it was already irrelevant to my goals. I published a fair amount in the amateur science fiction press, the fanzines, and these efforts were important to me because I got feedback about them. Soon enough, though, I lost interest in this whole side of writing. When I began to think seriously about poetry, I learned to think seriously about fiction too. The first story of any interest that I wrote came along in my senior year. As a story, it was dreadful, and I was wise to toss it away just as soon as I put a period in the final sentence. But it was lousy because it tried so hard, because it was original without attempting novelty, and because it was attached to a vision, one that I could not hammer into verse, no matter that this vision was the stuff of poetry, the real stuff, and probably not fit for fiction.

The vision I had was of seven marauder horsewomen in a snowy storm-whipped landscape. The women wore clothing patched together of animal skins and were barelegged and not at all clean. Their long hair streamed in the wind, blonde and greasy. Their horses were tall, white and black and dapple gray. These women preyed upon the hamlets and small settlements tucked away in the icy fastnesses and in the saddlebag of the leader was the severed head of a man, a poet who once had dared to become her lover.

This vision was important to me for reasons I've never tried or cared to understand. If I made a losing job of the story, too bad. The necessary thing was that I recognized in it a subject imperative to write about. As soon as I junked it I began another story, this one about an adolescent boy troubled by vivid fantasies that enmeshed completely his real life and were beginning to disorder his mind. The vision was important, but more important was *stepping back* from it, finding a dramatic context that would give it meaning. I learned in those hours to subject my vision to analysis and to make analysis part of the visionary process. The vision was incomplete without analysis, but without vision analysis was pointless.

I didn't know then what I had learned, of course, but I knew that I had learned something. When I packed up to go to the university that story (from which the marauder women had disappeared) and a sequence of villanelles about farm life went into the suitcase. All the other writing of the five years past, hundreds of pages, went to a bonfire, without lament and without ceremony.

Welcome to High Culture

When we think how many people it takes to produce one writer—how many tolerant relatives, gracious teachers, forbearing friends, and imposable strangers—it becomes obvious that the end product is not worth all the effort. But then, what is? It takes just as much warmly disinterested effort to turn out an athlete or a scientist or a responsible citizen. The State is going to spend the money anyway, those merry folk who have patience with young people are still going to be amenable; so that we may consider the appearance of a poet or fiction writer as an unexpected bonus, as the civilized world always has done.

Usually, though, the first serious encouragement that greets a writer is well-intentioned discouragement. "Writing," said my high school teachers, "is a good hobby, something you'll always be able to do. But don't expect to be successful at it. Most aspiring authors never get published." My parents saw the prospect in an even gloomier light, or darkness, than my teachers. Most of my friends thought I was certifiable for the mental wards, or was striving to become so.

It makes no difference. If a writer is going to write, he writes; if he does not write, then he is no writer. I didn't know what I was supposed to do with the first poems I wrote at ages twelve, thirteen, and fourteen. I buried many of them in the bottom cornfield, returning them to the soil I felt had given them birth. Others I placed on wood chips and, after setting

---

From *An Apple for My Teacher,* ed. Louis Rubin (Chapel Hill, N.C.: Algonquin Books, 1987).

them afire, floated them along the turgid currents of Duckett's Creek. I watched them drift out of sight, feeling jubilant and forlorn at the same time. . . . Such grandiose self-pity neither helped nor harmed the feverish lines on the Blue Horse notebook paper.

But—thank you, Mrs. Kellett. Though you never lodged the fourth declension in my disordered head, you showed me that others besides myself could be excited by books. I haven't forgotten the story of your becoming so absorbed in Dickens by lamplight that the room filled with smoke and you never noticed.

Thank you, Bill Anderson and Fuzz Fincher. It was good to have high school friends who thought that I was only immensely silly and not raving lunatic.

Thank you, Tom Covington, wherever you are, whatever course of life you pursue. I never learned to write a proper science fiction story suitable for those magazines, but you did manage to teach me to write a straightforward sentence, a comprehensible paragraph. I can still recall my astonishment when you broke off our correspondence upon joining the Navy; I had pictured you as a wise old man, in his thirties *at least.*

Once having opened the Catalogue of Debt, writers, even the most regretful and bitter among us, could go on and on and on, like the tearful young ladies in the Academy Awards ceremonies, until our audience too would cry out, "Say, didn't you do *anything* yourself?"

And that question ought to be taken seriously. Writing is such an inescapable part of literate culture, such an ordinary part of communal aspiration, that a writer should not much pride himself on his precious volumes. Even if he is the most radical of thinkers, someone who desires to tear his culture down and build it again from the bottom up, society—American society, anyhow—can turn to him and say, "Yes, but the reason you were educated was to enable you to think precisely these thoughts." The radical writer in America is stuck with this anomaly, that his only audience is the literate Establishment, who are by and large a broadminded and tolerant bunch. This fact makes him fight the band that heeds him.

Because one of the guildmark characteristics of a young

writer is self-dramatization, it may be that many of the early slurs and snickerings he endures are partly imaginary. A writer seems to feel instinctively that it is necessary to have something to struggle against, and I have met no writer, even among best-selling novelists, who did not believe that this reviewer or that one was out to get him, that his publisher has not advertised him lavishly enough, that his agent is an economic simpleton. This attitude of aggrieved affront may be a holdover from the years when none of the heartbreakingly pretty cheerleaders sufficiently adored his sonnets. Or it may come down to the other fact that writing is an inevitable part of culture, that a writer owes too much to too many, that at last he does have little for which he can take personal credit, and all this makes him uneasy and defensive. For no matter how many Miltons, Chekhovs, and Prousts have appeared or shall appear, the writer in the end remains what he was in the year 6000 B.C.—the village scrivener, a clerk.

Perhaps the cruel world is aware of this fact, perhaps that is why it gives him such a hard time. The village vests a heavy responsibility in its scrivener, who is to draw its portrait, preserve its memories, and keep its accounts, both material and spiritual. Perhaps the world is careful to weed out those not nervy enough to do justice to the office. If the writer prefers to impute motives of heartless jealousy, that is only more instance of his trying to make himself look good to himself.

But then he has to look good to himself, since to everyone else he looks merely odd.

College! I thought. If I can ever graduate from high school and get into college, I'll find kindred spirits, other people who will sympathize with my aspirations and respect my goals. I had heard of the legendary teacher of creative writing at Duke University, Dr. William Blackburn (though I thought his name was "Blackstone"), and I was confident that I was the student he had been praying to come along. I had given up science fiction and had recently written two heavily symbolic stories that were so mythically sophisticated I couldn't understand them. I was just hell on symbolism, and I felt certain that Dr. Blackstone would appreciate these superior endeavors.

I got into Duke all right, though it is not clear how I did—

not on the strength of my high school grades, surely. There I found out that freshmen were not allowed into the writing class. I would have to get through my first year, making passing grades in my physics and logic classes, before I was eligible to be admitted to the sanctified novitiate. And then I would have to submit a manuscript that met favorably his iron scrutiny.

A year, that year, it seemed to me, would be ten eternities coupled together like boxcars. I would shrivel and die, scarab beetles would gnaw my dessicated bones tangled on the chair and writing desk of my dormitory room, before that year passed. What in the world was I to do in the meantime?

I drank a great deal of beer and whiskey, and I wasn't very expert at it.

And there was a literary magazine, *The Archive,* which was the oldest college literary magazine in the United States, and had, among my convivial unliterary buddies, the reputation of being the dullest publication the Lord ever suffered to plummet from the presses. "Dull, is it?" says I. "*Archive,* your nondescript days are past. Here comes Fred Genius with his stories and poems to set you zooming the glittery avenue to international acclaim."

Then another obstacle presented itself. *The Archive,* I found out, had an editor. If the editor liked your material, he published it; if he didn't publish it, he returned it with a note explaining why it was unspeakable garbage. This editor's name was Reynolds Price. He was a straight-A senior, and he was, by all accounts, nobody's fool. Other undergraduates spoke of him with contempt, of course—in the way they spoke of all the literary crowd—but with *awed* contempt.

The most interesting revelation was that he was a flesh-and-blood human being like anyone else one might run into on campus. My experience with editors was that they were sinister spectral entities who occasionally scribbled crabbed notes on little blue rejection slips: "Your exposition is silly"; "This is not how Martians talk to each other"; "The pace of this story is like a Boy Scout hike—half trotting, half dawdling." But Reynolds Price was a student like myself. . . . Well, no, he certainly wasn't that; but he did live in a room on the third floor of the Independent Dormitory. My first obvious step toward making *The Archive* a famous magazine would be to accost this man and flash my blinding credentials.

I got cold feet. What if I wasn't such hot stuff as I'd been telling my shaving mirror? What if I was an ignorant hayseed from a farm three miles outside of Canton, North Carolina? What if Reynolds Price decided to talk in French? What if—what if, after all—what, O God, if I wrote badly?

I had already made friends with the deeply pondering, slow-talking poet James Applewhite, and I confided my plan and my fears to him, delighted to discover that he had considered the same plan and had nursed the same fears. We decided to pool our courage and face the wizard together.

The pool of courage we resorted to was an unwise quantity of beer and cooking sherry. Our evening of destiny started early and got late quickly, but when we felt we had girded ourselves sufficiently, we returned to campus and stumbled up the narrow stairs. We pounded, lurching, on his door and Reynolds let us in.

Into, it seemed, an entirely different universe. Our rooms in the freshman dormitories suddenly seemed a thousand miles away, those rooms with the mimeograph-paper green walls and bare, pocked linoleum-tile floors and for decoration only the naked, inscrutable smiles of Hugh Hefner's pinup girls. Reynolds's room was another kind of place. It was agreeably lit with lamps, not with those bald overhead lights found in dormitories and police stations. There was a rug on the floor; it wasn't large or expensive-looking, but it meant that we didn't feel we were hiking a chopblock when we crossed the room. On the walls were *framed* reproductions of Botticelli and Blake and Matisse, on his desk a miniature of a classical torso. A record was playing—Elisabeth Schwarzkopf, I think—and there was an autographed photo of her on the wall.

"Hello, jerks. Welcome to High Culture," Reynolds said.

—No, he didn't. He couldn't say those words, or think them in an eon of trying. Yet I had the fleeting but certain conviction that he was entitled to say them.

In fact, he was polite and cordial, much more so than the situation warranted. Reynolds has almost always managed to maintain a smooth and pleasant demeanor to match his pleasing looks, and I hope that his easy manners have always worked as sturdily in his service as they did during that awkward evening. He treated us amiably, with a reserved humorous gravity, no doubt having sized up our unsober conditions. We sat—that is, we collapsed into chairs—and he sat, and we attempted conversation.

Reynolds talked then just as he does now: fluently, nonchalantly, knowingly, allusively, and always with a partly hidden humor. His manner was so assured that we began to question the impulses that had brought us here, and our defensiveness returned to bully us worse than before. Jim and I began to pretend to talk more to each other than to our host, dropping scraps of poetry and code names, *Pound, Eliot, Hart Crane, Rimbaud.* The friendship of young writers is usually marked by this cryptic patter; it is as if they feel themselves members of a spy ring. But Reynolds picked up our hints.

The horribly deflating thing was that he not only picked them up, he bandied them easily, as if these subjects which had cost Jim and me so much trouble to find out about were the common and legitimate coin of social intercourse. That was a blow. There are always writers or certain kinds of writing that other, especially young, writers feel proprietary about, and I have watched even famous poets and novelists turn mildly belligerent when someone else in the room evinced knowledge of works which they have decided belong, godammit, only to them. But here was Reynolds Price, cheerfully, blithely, opining right and left in territory where Jim and I felt we had, if not first claim, then squatters' rights, at least. He made it worse by being invulnerable; it was clear he had actually read the stuff he talked about.

That fact ought finally to have made us furious, but it didn't. Reynolds's insouciance began to work a calmness upon us, and we began to relax a little, to enjoy ourselves. We began to welcome the discovery that here was someone else who was *one of us.* It got to be time, and long past time, for us to depart, and there was little pleasure in walking back through the mazy halls to the freshman dormitories. My position in life seemed grubbier to me than ever before, and I made stiff resolutions to change myself.

I could not change my life and it later brought me to minor disaster and major embarrassment. But that was not Reynolds's fault; he did the best he could with me, and it is astonishing to me now that a young man of twenty or twenty-one could have so much cheerful patience with a prickly adolescent only a few years his junior. There is a patience which is born of experience, but there must also be a patience born of innate wisdom, and it is this latter that Reynolds was graced with.

I began to bring him my work to read, long arcane poems and wild confused stories. I have mercifully forgotten this material by now, and almost all that I remember is Reynolds's good-natured meticulous attention as he went with a pinpoint-sharp pencil over line and line, word and word. His queries and objections on the page were delicate little breathings of graphite. This is how Rilke must have read through manuscripts, I would have thought—if I'd known who Rilke was. Sometimes he would use technical terms to criticize rhythms and tropes and I would never admit that I didn't know what those terms meant. "Ah yes," I said, nodding. "I see." Thinking, What in the name of seven sunken hells is an amphibrach?

He must have admired my persistence, at least. There was one longish, heavily Eliotic, tainted poem that I brought to him some dozens of times. Was it about a mystic nun? I can dimly recall only some image about a stained glass window. I must have written that poem forty times, following his intimations and encouragements. It never worked out. Finally I wrote an ugly parody of it, then gave up. And there were many other pieces to which we gave the same treatment. I spoke loudly and quarrelsomely in their favor; he argued gently and reasonably against certain passages. Little by little I would mollify and acquiesce at last.

He was never wrong. He wasn't always right; he was sometimes unable to diagnose the *exact* illness of a passage, and he would sometimes object to certain phrases and subject matter out of inevitable and necessary personal prejudice. But he was never wrong; his objections made logical, if not always artistic, good sense; or they appealed to some separate standard I'd never heard about or to some authority unknown to me.

(Who, pray tell, was Herbert Read? Who was Geoffrey Scott?) It didn't matter whether he was right or not; it was too important that he was never wrong.

I learned a great deal, perhaps as much about literature as I ever learned from anyone. I trudged to the dictionary and looked up *amphibrach,* to the library and checked out Read and Scott. Mostly I picked up knowledge simply by contact, the way the cat in the weedy field picks up beggar's-lice and Spanish needles. I learned that even the pantheon contemporary writers were living sinful creatures like me and the postman. Reynolds possessed a kind of movie-fan worship of writers and loved to collect gossip about Auden, Faulkner, Welty, Hemingway, and he loved to pass it on. These tidbits must have been special fun to pass on to a wooly kid who would sit openmouthed to hear about William Empson's toping habits.

He published a couple of his own stories in *The Archive.* They were good stories, appearing later in his collection, *The Names and Faces of Heroes.* Strange that they did not influence my fiction, because I certainly admired their accomplishment. But maybe it was already clear to me that Reynolds and I were headed in different directions. There seemed to be a tacit agreement that I was to be intense and wild and experimental, while he was to be traditional, Olympian, and successful.

Everyone who knew him took his eventual success for granted, and "eventual" was assumed to be only a few short years off—as indeed it was. Reynolds took a Rhodes scholarship, as we all knew he would, and impressed the powerful literary figures at Oxford, just as we expected him to do. "A Chain of Love," the longish story he wrote for Dr. Blackburn's class, Stephen Spender published in *Encounter.* Reynolds then returned to Duke as a freshman composition instructor and wrote his first novel. *A Long and Happy Life* was published to lucky, but well-deserved, wide acclaim. Here was his picture in *Time* and on the cover of *Saturday Review.* His carefully planned career seemed to have flourished exactly on schedule, and this fact occasioned some inescapable natural resentment, even from me. Maybe especially from me.

There were some gruff times between us at this period, but in the end they didn't matter. My gratitude was larger than, though perhaps for a while not as fierce as, my jealousy. I never forgot what I owed to Reynolds, and if I ever do I shall have become someone the human race ought to cease speaking to. Sometimes I've wondered if others have remarked the Goethean qualities about the man, his steady adherence to the highest ideals, his immense easy knowledge of all the civilized arts, his cultivated ease. It is an index to his character that if he reads these present lines, he will not be embarrassed, however much he may disagree with what they say.

There were others besides Jim and me for whom he was mentor. There was the poet Wallace Kaufman and the novelist Anne Tyler, and there must be many others of whom I am unaware. Their memories of Reynolds will differ vastly from mine, and yet I can't help imagining that their essential experiences of him as friend and teacher must be like mine in general outline.

He was, you see, a genuinely cultured person, and there are precious few of them in any situation, even in the universities. If you happen to entertain the fantasy, as I once did, that these figures are to be met with only in novels or history books, then you will be pleasantly shocked to meet one as a friend. It marks us when we do; it refreshes our ambitions and reillumines our sensibilities; it warms, for a longer time than we expect, our cooling existences.

In order to conclude in proper fashion this excursion into heartfelt sentimental nostalgia, it has occurred to me that I ought to drink a glass of wine in honor of Reynolds Price. What is needed is a rich, red, full-bodied wine, with an earthy but not harsh aftertaste, a rather soft finish. There is no drink like that in the house and I shall have to go to the wine shop, describe to the proprietor what I'm looking for, and ask his advice.

That is the difference between us, of course. Reynolds would know the correct vintage and the best year.

The Function of the Poet

To ask the question is to answer it—on one level, at least. After that, the subject becomes complicated.

What is the function of the poet?

—Why, to write poems, of course.

And how does he go about performing this act?

First he determines that he has something to say. Then he decides upon the best way to say it, and after that it is only a matter of intensive clerical labor, interrupted by desperate momentary surges of inspiration. It is rather like working next to a lamp with a faulty switch; the light keeps flickering from dim to bright, but never quite goes out. . . . Except when it does.

But that first step is likely to be the steepest. How does he find something to say? And when he thinks that he has found a promising subject, how does he decide that it is genuine and that he has anything to add to what centuries of poets have already said? For he knows very well indeed that there is no original subject for poetry any more than there is a new and original human emotion that he can feel and which no one else has felt before.

This guaranteed lack of originality is at once the poet's burden and his comfort. He recognizes that he must find new approaches to old subjects, that he must find new combinations of words and new arrangements of such poetic materials

---

Presented as a lecture at Roanoke College, February 15, 1990, under the sponsorship of the Center for Church and Society and the Jordan Endowment. It was subsequently published by Robert Denham.

as rhyme, meter, caesura, and metaphor; but he can take heart from the fact that other people have felt the same emotions that he proposes to arouse or to recall with his poem. They may not have been able to articulate these feelings or even to know exactly what it is that they have felt, but he counts terribly on the brotherhood of man, on the consonance of human sympathy, in order to arouse these feelings again in his audience, to define and to refine them, and if possible to ennoble them. And he cannot cheat: he cannot casually trigger the same well-trained neural responses that advertisers, demagogues, and sloganeers have so often used and abused.

The poet discovers something to say by putting himself in position to discover it. "Chance favors the prepared mind," said Louis Pasteur; and this proposition determines the poet's regimen: to learn to observe, to become friendly with the tools of his craft, to attempt to understand his own mind and his behavior, to feel continually the contours of experience. Then something is bound to happen that has a poem in it or about it. In fact, such events are taking place all the time, even in the poet's purview, but he is not always receptive. The kind of attention that the inception of a poem requires is not always accessible. Randall Jarrell's comparison, that a poet searching for a poem is like a man standing in a field during a storm, hoping to be struck by lightning—not once but many times—is an apt one. But it is easy to see how such as effort is bound to take its toll.

The emotions the poet feels are the same ones we all feel and often upon the same occasions. He is elated at the onset of spring, during parades, while falling in love, upon getting a raise in salary, at the opening of baseball season, at weddings. He is sad at funerals, during the breaking up of love affairs, upon the disappearance of a species of animal or plant from the earth, at the prospect of continued suffering and injustice among the nations, at the continued exploration of the bottomless abyss by his favored baseball team. The difference between the poet and the rest of us is that he must say something more eloquent than "Hot dog!" when he feels good and "Oh phooey!" when he feels bad.

And there is where the difficulty lies.

He is going to delineate, dramatize, and heighten a simple emotion by the use of complex means. He is going to attack this feeling, or surround it, or seduce it, with his words. He must choose a form and a manner in which to ply his blandishments upon his subject matter, and how shall he meet this new girl of his dreams? Will she be attracted to him by the patched and faded blue jeans, the torn T-shirt, the rebellious punk haircut of free verse? Or will she more readily disclose her beauties to the man in white tie, top hat, and regular meter? Or to the soft spoken humorous gentleman in the tweed jacket which disgorges from its breast pocket a blue-iris-colored silk handkerchief bearing a scent of gardenia?

There is no way for the poet to know the answer to this question. Yet he has to make a beginning. If the poem he wishes to write is a love poem, he is acutely aware that there is a long and bulky tradition of love poetry peeking—or glaring—over his shoulder, and he must decide how he wishes to position himself in relation to this tradition. If he finds in his feelings for the beloved a certain complexity which prevents the full-throated celebration of joy—so that he cannot simply sing like the birdies sing—and that there is a firmness in the texture of his thought, then he may well choose the sonnet as the form which is most fitting to his thought and to the urgent impulse behind it. Having chosen to write a sonnet, he knows where he stands in relation to the long tradition of love poetry. It may not be the most comfortable position because he has put himself in competition with Elizabeth Barrett Browning and George Meredith and Robert Lowell and Longfellow—and now that we think about it—with Shakespeare and with Dante. If it were a foot race, he would feel the encumbrance of a ball and chain.

He may decide to eschew the sonnet and to begin instead with a line of poetry that stretches in capital letters all across the page a string of obscene epithets testifying in one fashion or another to his passion, or at least to his virility. This is to say, he has chosen the radical rather than the traditional mode of verse. Perhaps he believes that he has chosen the modern over the ancient. But of course the modern is in a sense already ancient; it too is a tradition and he finds that he is in competition with Allen Ginsberg, Blaise Cendrars, Clayton Eshleman, and Robert Creeley. These poets too offer some mighty tough competition. And, to make the situation worse, he still has not escaped competition with Dante and Wordsworth and Shakespeare. They are still there and their presences now seem more than insurmountable; they look positively glowering.

Nevertheless, he is going to write his poem. It is in him to write, and he fails himself and the poem if he does not attempt to set it down. He picks up his pencil with a mixture of feelings difficult to describe and impossible to analyze, but he does feel—when the work is going as it ought—one thing quite clearly. "This is what I was born to do," he thinks.

He knows that poetry is what he was born to do because, like all the rest of us, he has to do a lot of things he was not born to do. It is incumbent upon each of us if we strive for contentment in our lives to be happy in our work. My Uncle Fudd used to tell me to try to be the best there ever was. "I saw you installing linoleum the other day," he said. "If that is what you're going to do you should try to be the best linoleum installer in the world."

All right, Uncle, I'm willing to try. But nothing is going to make me say that I was born to install linoleum. Linoleum installers, unlike poets, are made, not born.

That is the poet's first and last rationale for what he does. He writes poetry because he cannot help it. The discipline of poetry is lodged as securely in his body as an athlete's talent is lodged in his rather more comely body. And he justifies his existence in part by remembering that there are societies upon the earth without the use or even the concept of money, without the concept of athletic competition, even without a clear concept—according to the anthropologist Bronislaw Malinowski—of fatherhood. But there is no society of human beings, in past record or in present view, that lacks the concept and practice of poetry. Poetry is an activity, or way of thought, or habit of language, that is built into the human physiology.

And this fact makes it a little easier to get past the first and highest hurdle: the necessity of having inescapably to be a poet.

Now, having faced up to his destiny and produced his poem, what does our little man do next?

Why, he looks all about for someone to admire his work.

This situation is the more intricate one. The poet may have been born to produce poetry, but no one in the course of human time ever felt that he was put upon the globe in order to read poetry. It is a catch-as-catch-can proposition, this search by a poet for his audience.

He is not going to find much of an audience. He knows that already because it is historically—perhaps prehistorically—a part of the poet's predicament. The ancient Greek poet Callimachus and the Roman Horace after him both proclaimed their contempt for the vulgar crowd that simply did not appreciate their fine and clever words. *Odi vulgus,* they wrote: "I hate the mob." Milton wrote for fit audience though few. Whitman found a nifty way out by declaring that every man is his own poet and that he, Walt, had no more claim to be listened to than anyone else we might meet in the street. But this attitude is only the obverse of that of Horace and Milton, and the only people who know what Whitman's sentiments are in this regard already read the poems in which he outlines them.

Another solution to the problem of audience was broached by William Butler Yeats. Disgusted by and contemptuous of the middle class he found to be lacking in proper interest in poetic genius and nationalist literature, he decided to invent his audience, to write for an ideal reader. Yeats's ideal reader was of course an Irishman; he was also a fly fisherman, a man who gave up his whole attention to the art of casting flies, who went out at dawn each morning to practice his art. He describes him as "a wise and simple man," and vows to write for him "one / Poem maybe as cold / And passionate as the dawn." But he admits, is forced to admit, that his fisherman in gray Connemara cloth is "A man who does not exist, / A man who is but a dream."

Yeats's solution, ambiguous as it is, probably represents the way most contemporary poets resolve the problem of audience. The poet writes for a single ideal reader or for a small group of sympathetic readers. These latter may or may not exist in reality. He hopes for a larger number of readers and he knows that they do not exist—or that they exist only as scholars, for whom his poems are not regarded as poems so much as raw material for the profession of literary scholarship. The poet himself is perforce a scholar—of literature, of science, of politics, of any number of specialties—and he thinks with dismay of the kind of operation contemporary scholarship may perform upon his verses.

It was Yeats who also wrote the line, "Tread softly because you tread on my dreams." That is the kind of attitude that gets no sympathy from reviewers and critics, much less from scholars. Literary scholarship has become the kind of business it never was before in the western world, and as the personal motives of scholars become more selfish, so do their analytic methods become clumsier. Trying to tread softly with deconstructionist criticism is like trying to perform an entrechat while wearing snowshoes. The poet knows this disheartening fact, that his most careful readers will be critics afflicted with the virus of some strain of exotic theory. So how does he deal with that knowledge?

If he is wise he ignores it or forgets it. But we are not always wise. Sometimes he may try to outfox the professional critic. If a critic is learned, why then a poet too can be learned: he can seek out abstruser theories written in more obscure languages than ever a critic has dreamed of. He can build his poem on matrices of fractal geometry, borrow rhyme schemes from Provençal dance forms, and decorate them with allusions to Cambodian architecture. He can publish the poems with a flourish of his hand that seems to say, "There you go, buddy. Try to figure that one out!"

But this is a lost cause. The poet is a single person, writing one poem, no matter how lengthy or complex he makes it. The critics hunt in packs and time is on their side, as well as the traditional academic resources. Someone in the future is likely to pay them money for flushing the poet's errors and trivialities and even some of his achievements out of hiding.

So if the poet knows that scholars are likely to make up the largest number of his immediate audience, he tries to hope that this will not always be the case, that readers with less specialized interests will come to his work at last and evince a different kind of appreciation, an interest more personal and perhaps more aesthetic in nature, and less colored by merely professional concern.

But he can find this audience only if he is willing to satisfy its expectations. The poet thinks he knows what his readers want from him: his duties, as they have been defined over the millennia, are stable. The first responsibilities of the poet are to teach and to delight. Or, putting it in proper formulation: to teach by delighting. People come to his poems in order to learn things that they did not know, or to be reminded of things that needed to be remembered in fresh fashion. They gain this knowledge or rejuvenate these memories because the poet delights them with his use of language. He makes everything sound like fun. If ever a reader wrote to a poet, upon reading his volume and closing it up, a letter that said: "I'm glad I read your book. I had a good time and I learned a lot," then the poet might well feel that his life had been justified and that he could retire from the vocation. He could not, of course; one can retire from a profession but never from a vocation. Yet he might feel that he had accomplished most of what he had set out to do in his art.

But he never gets a letter like that. Usually he gets a letter saying, "Dear Jim-Bob, I enclose a copy of that gruesome review of your new book that I told you about on the phone. As I said, I don't agree with a word of it, but I thought you ought to see it." Or a letter that says, "Dear Mr. Hotpoet, I am a junior at Ragweed High here in Raw Neck, Utah, and I have been assigned to write a paper on your work. Will you please write me a letter telling me what your books are all about and how you came to write each one, and could you please reply by return express mail as I have kind of let this paper slip and it is due real soon, like I mean real SOON." Or he receives a letter that says, 'Dear Mr. Birdbard, I don't read poetry, but I saw your name on a book in the store and want to know if you are any kin to the Birdbard family in Goosejuice, Oregon. My aunt Flimsy Thimble was once married to a Birdbard and she said they were a rum bunch. I was curious if you might be one of the Oregon Birdbards." Many letters like these and then a few others that deserve their own butterfly nets, but never ever a letter that mentions teaching and delighting.

The poet himself might have a difficult time justifying the old justification. Haven't those terms changed over the centuries? Have they not broadened? Or have they narrowed?

What is it that the poet can teach? Will not a prudent person go to his minister for moral instruction or to a philosopher for ethical enlightenment and ontological speculation? Will he not apply to the scientists to know about atoms, hummingbirds, and the motions of tides? For understanding of human character will he not open the books of Freud, Jung, and William James? For history he will go to historians. When he reads about these matters in the poet's works, is he not merely getting the words of the true experts in secondhand prettified manner?

This question puts itself in simple terms: Is there any subject besides himself and the art of poetry that the poet is qualified in this day and age to teach?

And as for delight—well, what kind of fun can the poet offer that has half the attraction of Nintendo? Or, come to that, a fourth? Make it a tenth. We shall not even mention the other activities that the poet must compete with: movies, recordings, concerts, sports, television, and driving about amiably in convertibles.

Maybe we can help the poet out by making some elementary distinctions. Let us propose that *to teach* is not the same thing as *to instruct.* There are some things we learn in order to know them and some things we learn in order to live with them. If you wish to learn how to drive a car safely or how to manufacture hydrochloric acid, then it will be better not to turn to books of poetry for instruction. But if you wish to know or to remember how it feels still to be in love with a person who has done you most dreadful wrong and to search desperately for a way to forgive that person so that you can go on loving, then Facts on File is no help, nor the IBM PC Computer Operator's Manual. We need to learn, probably, the basic skills of driving automobiles only once; the other lesson, how to feel and behave in a difficult love affair, we must learn again and again. Then we turn to poetry.

As we normally do in other situations.

I do not know how to report this next observation from my personal experience without seeming to gloat—which I most certainly abhor to do. I shall only say that it has happened more times than a few that people who have aggressively attacked the whole idea of poetry in my hearing or who have belittled me for practicing it have sent me their own poems to read and comment upon when they have been faced with personal catastrophes and sorrows and poetry has been unwillingly wrung out of them. The usual occasions are the deaths of family members or of close friends and the hymn-meter verses produced are genuine in feeling. Then, when the hurt hearts ease a bit and time performs its secret assuaging ministry these nonce-poets take up their old attitudes again and relish teasing me about my uselessness in society.

It is difficult for people to understand that the poet might have a function. I fly about our busy nation in airplanes fairly frequently. Sooner or later my seat-mate on the plane will ask me what I do for a living. For years and years I replied that I was a schoolteacher. A meaningful pause. Then: "What do you teach?" And trying to be truthful for a moment I would answer: "I teach English." Another pregnant pause—and then either one of these two replies: "I guess I'd better watch my grammar," or "That was my very worst subject in school."

This conversation deteriorates immediately, in my opinion.

These days I'm elderly and gray and paunchy and don't care much any more. When the shiny young executive looks up from his printouts for a moment to ask me what I do for a living, I say, "I'm a poet." Then comes the longest pause you could ever imagine; the Byzantine civilization comes and goes while this nice young man ponders. Finally comes his sentence, the phrase that enables him to turn back to his figures and bottom lines with equanimity, dismissing me and my concerns to Etruscan obscurity. "I suppose," he says, "there's not much money in that."

I might reply in turn, "Oh, yes and no. Some years better than others. Only pulled in half a mill last year, but this year looks pretty good." I never say that sentence, but I might with perfect ease. Everyone lies on airplanes. And anyhow, Willie Nelson could say it, after adjusting the numbers upward quite a bit. Mr. Nelson is a poet, after all. So are all the pop singers. They only write a different kind of poetry than book poets do and have slightly different goals in view.

It is easy to forget that we live—or drown—in a sea of poetry. Not only popular songs but advertising jingles, political slogans, mnemonic rhymes, street jive, and a hundred other activities are informed by the energies and formal usages of poetry. Television advertising has taken over from the surrealist movement of the 1920s and 1930s its wild imagery, its disclocated logic, its irreverence, and its shock value. Television has not managed to capture the innocent heart of that movement, but it has stolen its fruitful mannerisms right and left.

And we could trace with greater or less effort the various influences of poetry upon the popular arts and commerce and industry, and it would not be too difficult to make out a good case for the tyranny of literary aesthetics over American business practices. Even so, such influences are but byproducts of the poet's purposes and in large degree probably irrelevant to them.

For he is still most of all concerned with what his work can do within itself. He is still concerned with teaching and delighting. But he knows, and maybe he has had to learn again lately, that delighting and entertaining are not the same thing. It is true that weak poetry can delight us when it is put to music—we have already mentioned Willie Nelson. But the delight of serious poetry (even when it is humorous in nature) is of a different kind.

There is an intensity of purpose about it that more casual productions do not approach. And there is in it an enormous respect for its subject matter, so much respect that the techniques of more popular art forms are rejected as lacking in respect. And there is a corresponding respect for the intended audience of poetry that the popular arts do not try to match. The best serious poetry expects that its readers shall be warm and empathic personalities, with intelligence and taste and deep concern for the truth. Sometimes, in responding to these expectations, certain readers may take on some of these qualities, though I would not strongly suggest that fine literature has the power to transform for the better the character of its audience—not many of them, anyhow, and not for very long. The popular arts do not usually hold such respectful expectations about their audiences: they cannot afford to because such expectations must be met with great care and painstaking time must be spent in composition and construction.

It is this kind of respect that makes poetry suspect in the minds of many people. Its very seriousness makes poetry seem unserious. Mr. Ted Turner likes to advertise his Cable News Network as being the most important of television networks because it broadcasts news and nothing but news. Still we remain unconvinced, you and I. The news may be *urgent* now and then, or quite often, but it is rarely *serious.* If we really regarded the news as serious we would bind our newspapers in leather or cloth and preserve them in our shelves, publish our novels and poems on newsprint and throw them away weekly. But it is the other way round, of course, because we know what is serious. It is the very old news that Sophocles brings and the Gospel of St. Luke and *The Bridge* of Hart Crane. But, as Ezra Pound observed, these poets still bring news, whereas the latest dispatches from eastern Europe will be out of date by the time they arrive upon our shores.

One way that the poet attempts to teach by delighting is by leading his readers to appreciate the excellent qualities of one subject or another. It may well be that his girlfriend comes first to mind—or a rainbow, a daffodil, a bottle of wine, a painting. In fact, when we come to the objects of nature even the homeliest and most insignificant may serve as cause for meditative appreciation by the poet. Examples are myriad, but here is a little poem by Edward Thomas, called "Tall Nettles."

> Tall nettles cover up, as they have done
> These many springs, the rusty harrow, the plough
> Long worn out, and the roller made of stone:
> Only the elm butt tops the nettles now.

This corner of the farmyard I like most:
As well as any bloom upon a flower
I like the dust on nettles, never lost
Except to prove the sweetness of a shower.

There it is, as simple as ever we could wish, a celebration not only of the generally uncelebrated nettle, but also of the dust that settles upon it. We are not surprised by the poem, except by its modest excellence. It does, after all, what we expect poets to do, to find a new way to praise something of our lives, and a new object to praise. The delight an interested reader takes from the poem is out of all proportion to its length and the putative importance of its subject matter; and the delight is, as I can aver after long acquaintance with these eight lines, perennial. I never come to them without a sense of anticipation or leave them without a feeling of satisfaction.

And the only trouble with my experience is that it is I who report it. A poet is expected to respond warmly, thoroughly, and accurately to the poetry he reads. Perhaps it is seen as a part of his job to support the fraternity of poets in the way that doctors so famously support the medical fraternity.

What is wanted then is a reader who is not poet nor critic nor scholar who will respond as warmly to Edward Thomas's lines as I do and who will react as carefully. Are there such readers? At one time or another in a poet's career, he doubts that there are, for he never hears reliable report of such a legendary creature. The tree surgeon does not repair after supper to his copy of *The Faerie Queene;* the disc jockey does not interlard his hectic patter with allusions to *Piers Plowman;* the weary farmer does not give up his Superbowl Sunday to a fresh perusal of Shakespeare's sonnets. In fact, as soon as we suggest these individual possibilities they sound farfetched, silly.

Yet such readers do exist, and it is over a period of time that they make themselves known. It may take generations, but word does at last get out that Herman Melville repays at least as much as Longfellow the time it takes to read him. William Blake ascends to the ranks of the greatest English poets; Thomas Traherne is discovered and enjoyed; William

Faulkner is distinguished from Erskine Caldwell, Nathanael West from Horace McCoy. And at the same time the names of many of the proud are humbled and brought low.

A patient and secret cadre of readers is at work in this process, overcoming the vagaries of the popular press and the perversities of critical theory. Some of these readers are inevitably academics, steady scholars and teachers of benevolent and searching curiosity. There is a traditional intercourse among them wherein new ideas are tested and overlooked authors of worth are reclaimed. But there are other readers too, beautiful amateurs and skillful collectors of books, persons whose reading is wider than it is profound and more guided by love of adventure than by accepted critical opinion. These readers are almost completely immune to the fevers of contemporary fashions in reading, though they enjoy good new work equally with the older when they are certain they have found it.

These are the voluptuary taxonomists of literature. They read for pleasure, and the pleasure of reading has become so keen for them that they are eager but patient to discriminate, to enjoy as much as possible of every sort of literature, not merely the so-called respectable sort. They are able to immerse themselves in reading so earnestly, so longingly, that their experience of books is the best part of their experience of life, and finally these two experiences are joined as one, life and literature commenting upon one another at equal length and with equal authority.

I am so happily convinced that such readers do indeed exist that I have tried to draw the portrait of one of them. The poem is called "The Reader" and it is dedicated to my mother-in-law, Helene Nicholls:

The Reader

Beside the floor lamp that has companioned her
For decades, in her Boston rocking chair,
Her body asks a painful question of the books.
Her fingers are so smooth and white
They reflect the pages; a light

The color of cool linen bathes her hands.
The books read into her long through the night.

There is a book that opens her like a fan; and so
She sees herself, her life, in delicate painted scenes
Displayed between the ivory ribs that may close up
The way she claps the book shut when she's through
The story that has no end but cannot longer go.
It doesn't matter what the story means;
Better if it has no meaning—or just enough
For her to say the sentence that she likes to say:
Why do these strange folks do the way they do?

And yet they comfort her, being all
That she could never be or wish to be;
They bring the world—or some outlook of its soul—
Into her small apartment that is cozy
As the huddling place of an animal
No one is yet aware of, living in
A secret corner of a secret continent,
An animal that watches, wonders, while the moon
Rides eastward and the sun comes up again
Over a forest deep as an ocean and as green.

This poem is my picture of one kind of ideal reader and if I am asked whether I believe that such a reader actually does exist I shall not know how to answer. For the purposes of my writing, for the purposes of my teaching of literature, this attentive reader does indeed exist. After all, it is for these same purposes that I myself exist and when the time comes that I must inevitably give these purposes over I shall no longer exist in the same way that I do now. I shall be a different person and the world that I inhabit shall be much changed also. And not, I think, for the better.

Meanwhile—*allons, citoyens!* Let us keep scouting faithfully through the poetry books, the good old ones and the good old new ones. Because there are more things in heaven and earth than can be dreamed by the dullard, the barbarian, and the postmodern literary theorist. And not only more things, but better ones.

The Indivisible Presence of Randall Jarrell

I first met Randall Jarrell in the spring of 1964 at a party given by the poet Robert Watson and his wife, Betty. Among the other guests were Peter Taylor, his wife Eleanor Ross Taylor, Robert Lowell—whom everyone called "Cal"—and his wife Elizabeth Hardwick. The occasion was the annual Literary Festival at the University of North Carolina in Greensboro; actually, the Literary Festival was a tradition of Woman's College that had been carried over during the recent transformation of that well loved institution into its new and befuddled university status.

The liberal arts tradition at Woman's College always had been strong and nowhere stronger, perhaps, than in its hospitality to contemporary literature. Robert Frost was a frequent guest on campus; Allen Tate and Caroline Gordon were former faculty members; and each year brought visits from writers like Robert Penn Warren, Andrew Lytle, John Crowe Ransom, and Eudora Welty. Randall Jarrell, as a famous poet, highly respected critic, redoubtable novelist, and teacher of legendary persuasiveness, ought to have felt right at home in the institution.

By most account, he was comfortable in Greensboro. It is almost as impossible to imagine Jarrell without an academic setting as it is to imagine him an ordinary academic. Not that he was one of the famously cranky figures among literary academ-

From *North Carolina Literary Review* 1, no. 1 (Summer 1992).

ics; he was no John Berryman or Delmore Schwartz or Theodore Roethke, drunken and bumptious. In fact, when I talked to him at the party I found him a charming, humorous, ebullient person—a bit taken with himself, of course, but part of the rationale for a literary party is its opportunity for the poetic peacocks to spread their fans. He was in the company of his wife Mary and her friendly good looks so distracted me that I really didn't hear the poet's opening remarks. These were, I think, conventional welcoming cordialities; I was to join the UNCG faculty as an instructor in the coming fall semester.

But the conversation soon veered to literature. Jarrell had little store of small talk, or maybe he only set little store by it. (Mary, however, enjoyed a delicious copiousness.) When I asked about any new project he might be engaged upon, he reported that he was translating Goethe's *Faust.* Long time past I had read two translations of *Faust*—by the Victorian poet Alice Meynell and by Louis MacNiece—but had read them only cursorily, I'm afraid. My stammering ignorance did not dismay him in the least; he began to speak of the vicissitudes and pleasures of the job with an infectious enthusiasm and with another quality in his manner I found difficult to pin down. I think now that I would describe a large part of his social manner as *a searching earnestness.* He is still the only person I have known who spoke his literary opinions not as suggestions or oracular announcements but as incontrovertible facts, data so thoroughly established that Copernican astronomy might more plausibly find doubters.

He was not offputting; he was only extremely watchful and intent and he seemed to make no distinction between one's intellectual side and one's more personal nature. It might be better to say that the personal simply didn't count as much with him as the intellectual, that he might forgive your indiscretions, missteps, and blunders, but would never forgive an inept estimate of a play by Chekhov or a poem by Whitman.

He flashed prominent shiny incisors, wore a prominent gray and black and white beard, and when excited by currents of his thought would cock his head to one side and chatter. It was as if Nature had attempted a hybrid of mage, Christmas elf, and chipmunk and had despaired of the combination and would never attempt it again—for it was obvious to me, even upon a fleeting first encounter, that Randall Jarrell was one of a kind.

He laughed easily. His voice was a thin clear treble; a student once described it as "piping" when Jarrell "danced a poem around the room." The student was not speaking of Jarrell's recitation of his own work, but his saying lines by Hardy or Hopkins or Eliot in his class in Modern Poetry. For he was as legendary as a teacher as he was as a writer; students signed up for his classes in hopeful droves and departed them regretfully but gratefully. After his death in 1965 I inherited his Modern Poetry class and ten years later students were still quoting his classroom comments in their papers and examinations.

How could they have known what he said so long ago and in such a limited space as a classroom? That problem remains a mystery to me, but serves to point up how warmly he was revered as a teacher. He had to draw the students' respect mostly in his role as a teacher, I think, because no majority of the undergraduates would have read his poetry, though it was obvious from the battered copies of his work in the library that quite a few had tried him out.

But if they found the teacher—that is, Jarrell the person—attractive, they might well have found his poems attractive too. For one thing, he made evident even upon first acquaintance that the literary Jarrell and the personal Jarrell were indivisible. And he expected the same condition to be true of his friends and colleagues. If his poetry is intensely thoughtful, its melancholy reveries punctuated by odd memories and embroidered with quicksilver allusion, that was the tenor of his conversation also. He seemed to take the whole range of western literature as a sort of grand piano that his mind was continually fingering etudes upon. Some hours after you had departed his company you realized that one of his strange sentences had been a witty variation upon some proverb of Thoreau or some line of Laforgue—and then you began to wonder how much more of his conversation you had missed or misunderstood.

He wasn't performing for you—not exactly. Neither did you feel that you were merely present during an ongoing monologue, as one sometimes feels in the company of the feverishly brilliant. This dizzying display of wit and erudition was only Jarrell's brand of social intercourse; the poet was offering you the best of his mind and personality at every moment. What made an encounter difficult was that he had so much to offer; there was such a magnitude to take in that the attention first quailed, and then tired and despaired, and sometimes at last rebelled. Yet he was no exhibitionist.

That is, he did not labor to show himself off. He only offered his treasures (and I think he did regard them as treasures) as freely and generously as the mockingbird offers its songs; the light of attention attuned him and roused him to talk the way the moonlight excites the mockingbird in his famous poem. If allusions tumbled over one another in his conversation it was never because he was trying to impress but because he found that various contexts illuminated each other variously. He was continually dipping a handnet into history and literature and bringing up bright shiny-wet specimens, comparing and judging. New contexts freshened subject matter and so a conversation could become a kind of game. If it was not hard serious fun then it was not really conversation. Jarrell was a skillful tennis player and maybe conversation-as-tennis is the best metaphor to describe his discourse. Only he served so many balls at a time it was hard to return any of them.

His poems exhibit this trait. In the first nineteen lines of "An English Garden in Austria" we find these names: the Sun King, the *Athalie* of Madame de Maintenon, Saint-Simon, Leibniz, Metastasio, Rousseau, Ländler, the Baron Lerchenau from Strauss's opera, *Der Rosenkavalier,* and the castrato singer Farinelli. Such a catalogue compiled from a few lines is by no means unusual in Jarrell's work; many of his poems look at first reading to be such a dense tissue of allusion that there seems no possibility of discovering the character of the thought beneath so heavy an encrustation of learning.

But there *is* a subject for "An English Garden"; it is a poem about the rise and fall of romanticism and the ruin that its decadence has made of the contemporary world. In form it is the spellbound reverie of a well-educated and deeply concerned man, and the following fourteen lines comprise a sprightly history of romantic revolution:

> Then all the world
> Shifts to another gear: Count Almaviva and his valet
> Shake hands, cry *Citoyen!* are coffined by a sad
> Danton; assisting, Anacharsis Clootz—
> To the Mason's Funeral Music of their maker.
> And one might have seen, presiding among drummers,
> An actress named *Raison* (*née* Diderot).
> Meanwhile Susanna and the Countess sigh
> For someone not yet on the scene; their man of tears
> Retires, is rouged as Destiny: Rousseau
> Comes in as Cain, upon a charger . . . Instead of his baton
> This corporal carries *Werther* in his knapsack.
> He reads it several times, and finds no fault
> Except with Werther: he was too ambitious.

The poet didn't talk so allusively, of course, but the difference between his conversation and these lines is partly one of degree. His chat would flash from one topic to another, darting through the decades and centuries, through the poems, memoirs, and novels, like a rubythroat hummingbird on its nervous but purposeful quests. And as he spoke he regarded his listeners closely, seeming to gauge by response the character and intellectual capacity of his present company.

I believe that more often than his dazed colleagues recognized, his intentions were humorous. The similarities and contrasts his allusiveness turned up amused him and he could hardly hear the most innocuous sentence without hearing at the same time an ironic echo. Irony was not only his stock in trade as a poet, it was his normal element. In regard to irony most of us are amphibious; we can come out of the mode and live on unambiguous dry soil when we feel the need. But I am not certain that Randall Jarrell could do so; perhaps he was trapped in his ironies. Miles Davis, the jazz musician, once confessed that he heard music in his mind all day long, from minute to minute without surcease; he did not report whether the experience was pleasant or not. Is it not possible that Jarrell was continuously engaged in composing his dark ironic poetry, and that his conversation was informed by this confused and relentless process?

That was the unhappy fate of Ezra Pound and of Torquato Tasso.

I won't dispute the fact that many readers find such a barrage of allusion daunting and that a common contemporary response to lines like those quoted above is impatient irritation. The Elvis-Is-King generation of poets is now the dominant one, I suspect, and a number of fairly young poets blame poetry's current lack of popularity on earlier poets who had the unmitigated gall to employ their learning as a part of their style. Let me just set down the buzz word "elitist" as sigil of the character of their complaints and move on to address the virtues of poems like "An English Garden in Austria."

Jarrell wrote a number of poems in this vein: "A Girl in a Library," "The Knight, Death, and the Devil," "A Game at Salzburg," "A Rhapsody on Irish Themes," "Hohensalzburg," "Money," "The Memoirs of Glückel of Hameln," and others. These are *capriccio* poems, pieces in which many different elements are closely juxtaposed, their implications jostling one another sometimes noisily and sometimes discordantly. They may remind readers of certain paintings by Fragonard, certain drawings of Piranesi, in which architectural styles of different periods are set side by side to be gazed upon by pensive shepherds or ignored by busy fruit vendors or washerwomen. These poems serve as tropes for the reach and variety of western culture; the speakers of the poems muse upon their monumental surroundings with different degrees of personal involvement in moods plangent or gay or quizzical. In Jarrell's poems the discourse of books and pictures and statues and buildings and music impinges upon the characters and makes a real difference in their lives.

The central figures in his poems often think of themselves as being surrounded by cultural objects of one sort or another, artifacts that underline or help to determine the color of their thoughts and temperaments. The woman in "Next Day" moves from *Cheer* to *Joy,* from *Joy* to *All,* but finds the extravagant promises of these commercial brand names chillingly disappointing. The secretary on her lunch break visiting the Washington zoo thinks of the exotic saris of women from eastern embassies as "cloth from the moon" and so begins to daydream of a fantastic transformation like the one that climaxes Strauss's *Ariadne auf Naxos.* In "A Girl in a Library" the drowsy student is immersed in a cultural environment whose meanings she is oblivious to in the same way that one of François Boucher's vagabond mountebanks is ignorant of the history of the ruined Corinthian portico under which he has pitched his tent. One of the most thorough interdependencies between character and cultural milieu is that depicted in "The Night Before the Night Before Christmas."

The speaker of "A Conversation with the Devil" is closely involved with his cultural environment because, as a poet, he forms an active part of it himself. This is a fascinating and complex poem; a longish careful essay would be required to do it justice. It is at once a homage to Goethe's *Faust* and an amused farewell to its romantic melodrama; it is at the same time a parody of that story and of Thomas Mann's *Doctor Faustus,* presenting us the drama of the modern artist arguing with his own disease, the illness which is both his art and his life. It is also an exercise in self-mockery, a mode habitual in Jarrell's poetry and one that critics sometimes take at face value and deride as sentimentality.

"A Conversation" begins with the poet at work in composing his own epitaph. He complains about his lack of popularity and wonders if he ought to strike a metaphorical deal with the devil by writing the sort of stuff that can please a mass audience. The devil then appears to him and offers this diabolical advice:

> Lie, man, lie!
> Come, give it up—this whining poetry;
> To any man be anything. If nothing works,
> Why then, Have Faith.
> That blessed word, Democracy!

But Mephistopheles is only teasing, we discover, for the poet and the devil are already compact in a serious contract concerned with the length of the poet's life, just as in Marlowe's play and Goethe's:

> Our real terms were different
> And signed and sealed for good, neither in blood
> Nor ink but in my life: *Neither to live*
> *Nor ask for life*—that wasn't a bad bargain
> For a poor devil of a poet, was it?
> One makes a solitude and calls it peace.

As the dialogue continues it becomes obvious that the poet and the devil are not two separate figures but only two voices of the poet himself as he looks out upon the atomic age and wonders if both poet and devil are not mere mummeries, fustian relics of an outworn age. The devil calls the poet "a bored anachronism" and the poet acknowledges the justice of the description.

Playful and mercurial, "A Conversation" is at heart a darkly serious work, addressing the position of the poet in the contemporary world and his responsibilities. The poet is exhibited here not only as a representative of the intellectual caste but also as a representative of mankind as a whole. As a man he is able to defeat the devil in a paradoxical and unhappy fashion, but since he is first of all a poet and a man with human faults, the devil tempts him in personal terms. He offers him the opportunity to write a kind of poetry that will insure him mass popularity: "EACH POEM GUARANTEED / A LIE OR PERMANENTLY IRRELEVANT / WE FURNISH POEMS *AND* READERS."

This temptation is but a weak one; the poet sees through it immediately because it is one he has encountered often before and has always rejected. The voice of the devil in this temptation is the same as the voice Jarrell imagined for the mass audience of Americans who make mock of the philosophically inclined temperament in his 1959 essay, "The Intellectual in America":

> You highbrows, you longhairs, you eggheads, are the
> way you are because there's something wrong with

> you. You sit there in your ivory tower, pretending you're so different from other people, wasting your time with all these books nobody buys, and all these pictures my six-year-old boy can draw better than, and all those equations it takes an egghead like yourself to make heads or tails of—why don't you get wise to yourself and do what I do, and say what I say, and think like I think, and then maybe I'd have some respect for you?

These sentences might well stand as Jarrell's reply to our "now" generation of poets who so abhor any trace of learning in poetry. Their complaints would sound to Jarrell like the voice of the mass audience, the *profanum vulgus,* with its spurious blandishments—that is to say, like the voice of the devil himself.

It is only remiss schoolchildren who find learning a burden. Mature persons—particularly including mature poets—find it enjoyable and refreshing. And how can there be any poetry, except for the simplest lyrics, that is not tinged with some sort of learning? If we begin by barring American poets from alluding to Madame de Maintenon because many readers will not recognize her name, shall we not soon have to exile such names as Ty Cobb, Eli Whitney, Louis Sullivan, Jim Corbett, W. C. Handy and Francis Scott Key? Where shall we ever stop? It has traditionally been part of the pleasure of poetry that it remembers and celebrates our history and recalls to us passages of our heritage that we are fearful of forgetting. But if poetry is condemned to mumble a rosary of mass media names—Elvis, Madonna, Buddy Holly, Al Capone, Ronald Reagan—and to present this threadbare paucity as our cultural history, then it will become only a species of inferior television documentary.

Just as some of Jarrell's colleagues found his highly implicative conversation challenging, so some readers now find his densely allusive poetry threatening. The kind of threat it seems to pose is an obscure one; a Jarrell poem only lies there on the page, inviting readers but not physically accosting them. Yet for some people a poem like "A Girl in a Library" looks like a Gordian knot and their impulse is either to hack through it like the impetuous Alexander or to dismiss it as being merely a uselessly complicated lump of hemp.

Yet the structure of that poem is as easily got undone as a shoelace bow; it is only the speaker gazing at a girl trying to study in her college library and saying to himself—as a teacher will do—"I love you, I love you not," as if he were plucking the petals from a daisy. The surface of "A Girl in a Library" is a silver filigree of references, yet these comprise but a jolly mocking inventory of the furnishings of a professional mind. Richard Strauss, Kipling, Pushkin, Wagner, James G. Frazer—these savants are present not only for the sake of contrast; they make up the fairy-tale Dark Wood into which the innocent young girl has wandered. About the girl the speaker cannot quite make up his mind. "I love you—and yet—and yet—I love you," he says, and the sentence is spoken in that most familiar of a teacher's tones, fond exasperation. But about their historical relationship he has no doubt; it is traditional, as old as civilization itself. In fact, this relationship defines civilization, when the speaker begins to examine the figure of the girl in a social and anthropological context:

> One comes, a finger's breadth beneath your skin,
> To the braided maidens singing as they spin;
> There sound the shepherd's pipe, the watchman's rattle
> Across the short dark distance of the years.
> I am a thought of yours: and yet, you do not think . . .
> The firelight of a long, blind dreaming story
> Lingers upon your lips; and I have seen
> Firm, fixed forever in your closing eyes,
> The Corn King beckoning to his Spring Queen.

The girl has a primary role to perform in the rites of spring, the same rites that gave rise to the grand cultural edifice that encloses her. Stubbornly unintellectual, she still has an important place in intellectual history.

A churlish reading of "A Girl in a Library" can render it an insult to the young woman: she is so fecklessly dumb the only thing she is good for is reproduction, as she takes her place in the fertility ritual. But the countertheme of the poem, playing off the estrangement of the girl from her cultural history, is the speaker's estrangement from the girl and what she represents, an easy unselfconscious engagement with the pleasures and vexations of daily life. The girl and her teacher have a close relationship; they may even become friends, but their friendship will never be profound.

In September 1956, Jarrell wrote a chatty letter to Elizabeth Bishop that closes with a telling complaint. He is speaking about Greensboro: "Alas, Peter Taylor moved up to Kenyon from North Carolina—I don't have any really literary friends here, though several good ones of other sorts." This is not the utterance of a man plunged into dark despair; it is only a casual complaint that points up the same kind of loneliness that oppresses the speaker of "A Girl in a Library." Jarrell may have had many good friends of "other sorts," but it is clear that his only complete friends are the "really literary friends."

I must emphasize that the remark is casual: I don't want to read into it more than its suggestion that he regarded the unintellectual person as being deficient, incapable perhaps of the most precious kind of friendship. But I do want to point out that he is not complaining about the fact that his girl students are unintellectual, nor his barber, nor his tennis partners; he is talking about his colleagues, teachers whose profession is supposed to require them to be intellectual. At one time or another Jarrell may have been angry about the standards of American colleges (the majority of them, not just the one he taught at in Greensboro), but his anger at last subsided into a dazed chagrin. Yet his best response to the situation is not his vexed essays in *A Sad Heart at the Supermarket* and elsewhere, but in his comic novel, *Pictures at an Institution.* In the same letter to Elizabeth Bishop quoted above he defends it as being "a serious book," and it is that indeed—one of the most accurate and durable satires ever written about higher education in America.

His longing for intellectual company made Jarrell not only an inviting target for the usual self-complacent academic gossip but vulnerable to some instances of thoughtless cruelty. In the late spring of 1964 he could not prevent himself from holding forth at length in public on any occasion fit or unfit, and I watched as he stood on the campus talking to a group of students and faculty at a lawn party while one of his junior colleagues in the English Department teased him by proposing topics. "Turgenev," he would say, or "football" or "Wells cathedral," and Jarrell would come back with judgments and opinions, anecdotes and allusions, delivered in bursts of aphorism and fusillades of skewed wit. It was conversation-as-tennis gone out of control, and the younger man began to send over the invisible net the most ridiculous serves. "Rats," he said, and "wallpaper" and "shoes" and "doors," and the poet fought desperately to improvise something vivid and memorable about these subjects. I watched, fascinated, as the scene took place but did not understand what I was seeing. I must hope that if I had understood I would have found a way to stop the exhibition off.

But that scene only displays a symptom; it is not acutely informative. Jarrell was victim to a clinical condition that attacks many thousands and is of interest here only because he reacted to it in such a highly individual manner. He tried to alleviate his depression with the tools he had at hand, the instruments of his intellect that he had fashioned himself and had kept gleamingly bright. If these tools failed him that task, it is probably because they are never suited for it.

The propensity of contemporary biography and literary history and theory is to reduce the lives of poets and writers to case histories. Writers are but ambulatory diseases in this view, and criticism is prognosis. Yet such a view is only temporary, the product of a smugness that is markedly defensive in nature. Jarrell was aware of a more sensible view of the situation and in his essay "Poets, Critics, and Readers" put it in these words: "We all realize that writers are inspired, but helpless and fallible beings, who know not what they write; readers, we know from personal experience, are less inspired but no less helpless and fallible beings, who half the time don't know what they're reading."

But Randall Jarrell wrote for "the uncommon reader," as he tells us in "A Conversation with the Devil" ("I've some: a wife, a nun, a ghost or two"), the reader who was just as helpless and fallible as the human poet, but almost as inspired too. That, I believe, is what he desired from his friends and acquaintances—their best thoughts as well as their affections, their inspired minds as well as their faithful hearts.

The Longing to Belong

It is the dread question the interviewer never fails to ask: "Why did you become a writer?" The author sweats and stammers. He doesn't know why he became a writer. If he knew that he would know perhaps more than is good for him, certainly more than is good for his work.

But the novelist Jose Luis Donoso has a telling answer. Why is he a writer? "Because," he says, "I wasn't invited to the party."

His explanation is incomplete, of course, but it is neat, lacks self-aggrandizement, and encapsulates much of the theme of *Tonio Kröger.* And it points up the fact that the sense of detachment, even of alienation, which is indispensable for a writer is often established in childhood and that the memory of this alienation may remain powerful throughout a long literary career.

The child as outsider is an important theme in the poetry of Randall Jarrell, one that he returns to again and again. In fact, when we number those stages or conditions of our lives when we haplessly find ourselves social outsiders—as travelers, as invalids, as students or soldiers or refugees or elderly—we can note that Jarrell has treated of most of them with fine sensitivity. While some writers have welcomed and celebrated their status as outsiders—Shelley, for example, and Lermontov and Poe and Rimbaud—Jarrell has emphasized instead the loneliness and bewilderment and the feeling of abandonment.

There is in Jarrell's poetry the longing to belong to some

From *Field,* no. 35 (Fall 1986).

settled, established, and humane order of existence. There is at the same time a painful recognition that this sort of order does not, and probably cannot, exist in the world that we know. Yet still it ought to exist somewhere; it is a necessary Ideal, just beyond the fringe of the terrible Actual.

Jarrell would like to posit childhood as one part of this ideal order. He would like to describe childhood in the words with which Hölderlin describes it in his novel, *Hyperion:*

> Yes, divine is the being of the child; so long as it has not been dipped in the chameleon colors of men.
>
> The child is wholly what it is, and that is why it is so beautiful.
>
> The pressure of Law and Fate touches it not; only in the child is freedom.
>
> In the child is peace; it has not yet come to be at odds with itself. Wealth is in the child; it knows not its heart nor the inadequacy of life. It is immortal, for it has not heard of death.

He would like to think of childhood in these terms, but he cannot do so. Children in the twentieth century are familiarly conversant with death, and they are a long way from being immortal, and Jarrell dramatizes the true state of things in poems like "Protocols," "The State," and "The Truth." In "Come to the Stone . . ." the war victim child has imagined his epitaph: "*Come to the stone and tell me why I died.*" But no one can give him any better answer than his own terrified earlier question which he has formulated in a child's terms of the consequences of bad behavior. "The people are punishing the people—why?"

His fiction is another matter, but in Jarrell's poetry there is not, so far as I can find, a single portrait of a genuinely happy child. All the children in his poems—and there are a great many of them—are under attack by a world intent on robbing them of the experience of what the poet regards as a true childhood. Losing comfort, security, certainty, these children look toward their future lives—when they are to have any—with bewilderment and sorrow and sometimes with a skeptical weariness. In some near direction or other lies Childhood, but they have been barred from it.

A solid example of this kind of subject matter is the poem called "Moving." It is one of the simpler and quieter examples, and is perhaps the more effective because of these qualities. "Moving" consists of five stanzas of fairly regular iambic in irregular line lengths, irregularly rhymed. The three outer stanzas (the final one is a single line) are spoken by a sympathetic outside observer; the inner two stanzas are the interior monologue of a little farm girl, probably of a poor family ("A smeared, banged, tow-headed / Girl in a flowered, flour-sack print"), who watches as their belongings are loaded into a van when the family has to move to a new address. It is a disturbing experience for the child, and it is the only experience the poem deals with. The poem's economy is a necessary part of its pathos.

Moving

Some of the sky is grey and some of it is white.
The leaves have lost their heads
And are dancing round the tree in circles, dead;
The cat is in it.
A smeared, banged, tow-headed
Girl in a flowered, flour-sack print
Sniffles and holds up her last bite
Of bread and butter and brown sugar to the wind.

Butter the cat's paws
And bread the wind. We are moving.
I shall never again sing
Good morning, Dear Teacher, to my own dear teacher.
Never again
Will Augusta be the capital of Maine.
The dew has rusted the catch of the strap of my satchel
And the sun has fallen from the place where it was chained
With a blue construction-paper chain. . . .
Someone else must draw the bow
And the blunderbuss, the great gobbler
Upside down under the stone arrow
In the black, bell-brimmed hat—
And the cattycornered bat.
The witch on the blackboard
Says: "Put the Plough into the Wagon

Before it turns into a Bear and sleeps all winter
In your play-house under the catalpa."
Never again will Orion
Fall on my speller through the star
Taped on the broken window by my cot.
My knee is ridged like corn
And the scab peels off it.
We are going to live in a new pumpkin
Under a gold star.

There is not much else.
The wind blows somewhere else.
The brass bed bobs to the van.
The broody hen
Squawks upside-down—her eggs are boiled;
The cat is dragged from the limb.
The little girl
Looks over the shoulders of the moving-men
At her own street;
And, yard by lot, it changes.
Never again.
But she feels her tea-set with her elbow
And inches closer to her mother;
Then she shuts her eyes, and sits there, and squashed red
Circles and leaves like colored chalk
Come on in her dark head
And are darkened, and float farther
And farther and farther from the stretched-out hands
That float out from her in her broody trance:
She hears her own heart and her cat's heart beating.

She holds the cat so close to her he pants.

The time is autumn, between Halloween and Thanksgiving (an irony not insisted upon); the girl sits outside, watching her cat play in the windblown fallen leaves. Her weeping has been pacified with a homely sweet, and now she only "Sniffles and holds up her last bite / Of bread and butter and brown sugar to the wind." She holds the sugared bread up as a ritual offering, rather like a libation, trying to gain some sense of security with rituals both traditional and private. "Butter the cat's paws

/ And bread the wind. We are moving." There is probably an ironic echo here of Ecclesiastes: "Cast thy bread upon the waters: for thou shalt find it after many days."

The child in "Moving" is an exceptional little girl, and what she most regrets leaving is her grammar school. It used to be common for sharecropper or poor farm children to have the education they enjoyed and desired so often interrupted and disjointed that it amounted to no education at all. Novelists like Faulkner and Elizabeth Madox Roberts have written touchingly of the experience. Seven lines exhibit the girl's feeling of accomplishment and belonging and her sense of loss:

> I shall never again sing
> Good morning, Dear Teacher, to my own dear teacher.
> Never again
> Will Augusta be the capital of Maine.
> The dew has rusted the catch of the strap of my satchel
> And the sun has fallen from the place where it was chained
> With a blue construction-paper chain. . . .

The latter two lines introduce the strain of imagery of the wallboard pin-up display in the classroom, the imagery that characterizes her feeling of established order breaking down, of things coming apart. She will not be present to help finish the Thanksgiving display with its turkey and pilgrims and Indians. In a sudden brief flight of fancy, she identifies the paper cut-outs pinned to the wallboard with the constellations which look as if they were pinned to the night sky:

> The witch on the blackboard
> Says: "Put the Plough into the Wagon
> Before it turns into a Bear and sleeps all winter
> In your play-house under the catalpa."

Part of the poet's purpose here is to indicate the boundaries of the girl's universe, which is both enormous and minuscule at the same time; it encompasses the earth and the stars, but only in terms that are homely and familiar. The apocalyptic collision of the constellations, "the Plough into the Wagon," disorders her universe; but she would have observed a real plow loaded into a real wagon anytime that a new field was ready to be tilled. The natural order of things is so intimate to her that she has used one constellation as a reading lamp: "Never again will Orion / Fall on my speller through the star / Taped on the broken window by my cot." The natural order she has depended upon is smashed. These lines echo the poignant earlier lines which emphasize the fact that order has disappeared: "Never again / Will Augusta be the capital of Maine."

The conclusion of the child's train of thought brings in another of Jarrell's favorite themes, that of transformation or metamorphosis. In order to prepare for her new life elsewhere, she must shed her old life, as a snake sheds its skin. "My knee is ridged like corn / And the scab peels off it." The tactile association of the scab with seed corn on the cob, new seed to be planted in a new field, is a daring one and maybe a little strained—but it is muted. Jarrell, always a tactful poet, no more insists upon his subtler ironies than upon his more obvious ones.

The little girl's final thought is hopeful, or rather, wishful, and wraps up the three separate thematic elements—astronomy, her classroom and scholarly accomplishment, and transformation—in a single couplet alluding to the story of Cinderella. "We are going to live in a new pumpkin / Under a gold star."

Perhaps there will be a happy ending; perhaps this moving to a new place signals her family's magical transformation into a secure and happy one. . . . At any rate, she is mollified, she has found a fantasy that enables her to accept the hard facts of the real world.

The comfort she finds is almost certainly illusory. "One makes a solitude and calls it peace," Jarrell says in his poem "Conversation with the Devil," and that is what the little girl has done. But for the moment, for her, this comfort is sufficient.

The third part of the poem, however, with its shift to an objective outside observer shatters the warm tone of the girl's thought with an abrupt monosyllabic line: "There is not much else." It is an ambiguous line, pointing forward and backward at once: "there is little alternative in the way she *can* think," and, "there is not much left to report."

Jarrell then gives a series of literal details which in their disorder mirror the earlier phantasmagoria of the child's fancies:

> The brass bed bobs to the van.
> The broody hen
> Squawks upside-down—her eggs are boiled;
> The cat is dragged from the limb.

These events are reported in passive mood so that there seems no human agency responsible for them. The bed is not carried, but on its own "bobs" to the van. No one is holding the broody hen by her legs, she simply "Squawks upside-down," and her eggs, which were to be the beginning of a flock, have been boiled. The Halloween cat is dragged from the tree as if being unpinned and taken down from the classroom wallboard. The details are perfectly realistic, but, couched in passive mood and after the child's confused thoughts, take on an eerie unreal quality. The outer world of fact has become the unfactual world of her inner vision.

This is the real transformation, the true metamorphosis—very unlike the one in the Cinderella story—and the girl now recognizes it. The comfort of her momentary fantasy deserts her. She looks round her at the place she is leaving. "And, yard by lot, it changes. / Never again." She has lost belief in her fairy tale, "And inches closer to her mother." Now she makes one final desperate attempt to look into her future.

> Then she shuts her eyes, and sits there, and squashed red
> Circles and leaves like colored chalk
> Come on in her dark head
> And are darkened, and float farther
> And farther and farther from the stretched-out hands
> That float out from her in her broody trance:
> She hears her own heart and her cat's heart beating.

The young girl makes an unlikely oracle; she cannot foresee the future. She resembles a little the unsuccessful oracles in *The Waste Land,* but Jarrell's reference here is to Gerard Manley Hopkins's sonnet, "Spelt from Sybil's Leaves," and the mood is just as dark as in that poem. But again it is a muted reference; the image of the girl amid falling leaves both real and imaginary is effective whether Hopkins comes to the reader's mind or not. Yet the contrast between Hopkins's great dark figure at the end of her world and Jarrell's wistful heartsick farm girl at the end of hers adds an unexpected ironic overtone.

Her visionary attempt fails. For comfort and security the child has to return to the real things that surround her in present time. "She holds the cat so close to her he pants."

Now the direction in which Childhood lies is, for this little girl at least, entirely clear: it lies behind. "Never again." And it is as much a geographical place as it is a state of mind or a temporary condition of life. For in Jarrell's poems Childhood exists apart from the children: it is a sort of utopia from which they have been barred.

Exile is the theme of "Moving," just as surely as it is the theme of Jarrell's poems about refugees, displaced persons, and prisoners, and just as it is the theme of some of the poems about aging, like "Next Day." The Marschallin, "die alte Frau," of *Der Rosenkavalier* is a very different person indeed from the little farm girl; yet it seems inevitable that in her future life she will utter the same words that the Marschallin does in "The Face":

> This is what happens to everyone.
> At first you get bigger, you know more,
> Then something goes wrong.
> You are, and you say I am—
> And you were . . . I've been too long.

Gibbons Ruark

The Ambition for Simplicity

The ambition to live simply and quietly and gently requires a vision so different from the one our contemporary society encourages that we feel privileged by the presence of a poet who can hold to this ambition, who is not persuaded by opportunities for spurious celebrity to abjure the values that have sustained him as a poet and as a private person. Simplicity once again shows itself as one of the noblest goals of poetry and as one of the most difficult to achieve, now that the habitual disorder of current events is offered as justification for artistic incoherence.

As Gibbons Ruark reminds us in an elegy from his 1983 collection of poems, *Keeping Company,*[1] we have it on the best possible authority that quietness is one of the most beautiful of ideals: "Mozart is supposed / To have said something heartbreaking" about quietness in his last hours on earth.

The quiet simplicity of Gibbons Ruark's poetry is its best strength and its happiest attraction. Many of the nouns which can be mustered to describe this Mozartian kind of art, *grace, ease, poise, balance, steadiness, wholeness, patience, calmness,* and so forth, are to be found plentifully in the poetry itself, as if the poet wanted to make certain that his readers will know the goals he is aiming for, as if to reassure us that these qualities can still be attained if only they can be faithfully imagined.

Ruark comes by his love for quietness naturally. His father, Henry, was a Methodist minister and the poet's boyhood was spent in a series of parsonages in eastern North Carolina. Since 1968 he has taught at the University of Delaware, departing only to take sabbatical or vacation leave in Europe or Ireland.

His insistence on the virtues of simplicity and quietness, his efforts to reassure his readers that such virtues are still attainable even in noisy and chaotic times, give rise to the characteristic gestures of much of his work. In the title poem of his first book, *A Program for Survival,*[2] a science fiction fantasy is indulged, a visitation by a "monstrous flying thing from another / Planet that throbs and bristles with a thousand arms." How are the inhabitants of Earth to assuage this stranger who, being alarmed, might decide to protect itself by means of unreckonable force? By stripping off our clothes and making love en masse in its presence, the poem suggests:

> Let us lie down
> With our lovers when we know them, falling on them
> Softly as possible, rocking with them, getting
> Up and turning to the future humming in the grass.
> As the salt of loving glistens on our bodies,
> Let us admire ourselves in the mirroring surface
> While the machine is gentled and admires us all.

Thus the poem is revealed as being no fantasy. The monster flying machine that bristles with a thousand arms is the frightening mechanical civilization that one part of our human nature has constructed and to control it will need the employment of another side of our nature, the loving animal aspect that can enable us to gentle our machines.

The adroitness of Ruark's fable is likely to go unremarked. The jocular gaudiness of the fancy passes off in a short time, the thoughtfulness of the allegory shines forth for a moment and subsides, and the poem concludes with an enormous but warmly understated wish. It requires another short space of time to recall the surface details to mind, and a reader comes away not quite certain that he has read a poem in which a monster invasion from Mars has been deflected by a global sex orgy.

The narrative materials of "A Program for Survival" are humorously chosen and lie outside Ruark's usual range. His range is, in fact, deliberately a rather narrow one. Love for family members and friends is celebrated, and again and again their deaths are elegized; there are numerous love poems to his wife Kay; there are travel poems and poems about works of art and music and there are a few portrait poems of historical figures—and that's about the whole scope. A singular devotion to a limited number of subjects is another way of achieving simplicity in the body of work, even though the choice to limit may not be deliberate but made under compulsion of powerful feeling.

There are many poems about the poet's father, for example, who, according to the evidence of the poems, established and maintained a close warm relationship with his son. Ruark has remarked recently, in an interview with Harry Humes, that, along with his wife, the example of his father's "sweetness and composure" stands behind his work. One of the earliest poems, "Night Fishing," was composed during the father's lifetime but takes as its subject the inevitability of his death. In this poem father and son travel to the shore to enjoy surf casting:

> We have come again, my father and I,
> To the edge of the known land, to the streak
> Of sand that lips the undermining sea.

The father's figure in the dark, his stalwart presence, seems an unchanging stability; "My father stands like a driven piling." Yet we already know that the sea is an "undermining" force, and the pull of the tides of merciless time brings the two fishermen close together.

> Yearly we come to this familiar coast
> To wade beside each other in the shallows,
> Reaching for bluefish in the ocean's darkness
> Till our lines are tangled and our tackle lost.

The sorrow of the poem is all the more profound for being muted, and the sadness of the subject is all the more bitter for being a premonition rather than an actual fact.

When the death does take place, one of the poems that results is, characteristically, a reassuring gesture, an epistle addressed to the poet's mother. For her he will say "these words that do not matter / Or that matter more than anything I do."

Mother and son are reconciled to this death; they do not inconsolably cry out for the father's return, but they do long for him to come to tell them "how to take his leaving," to sit quietly with them, "Saying no more than I am for the sake / Of so much mildness gone out of the world" ("In Elegy, A Letter Home").

Ruark's second book, *Reeds,*[3] opens with "The Darkness of the Room," a poem which retains this same steady calmness in the face of sorrow, and displays Ruark's talent for easy, almost casual approach. The speaker finds himself in a nocturnal winter landscape, made uneasy by the snowy barrenness of nature, "a landscape // Emptier than any silence." He decides to go into his house and sit by the sinking fire which he will not build higher and say to himself

> What a child says
> To his sleeping father,
>
> I came down to kiss you
> Goodnight but it's so dark
> I don't know where your mouth is.

His gentle approaches and quiet closures also serve Ruark well in his love poems. Here are the opening and closing passages from two such poems, first from *Reeds* and then from *Keeping Company:*

> Lately I think of my love for you and the rose
> Growing into the house, springing up from under the eaves
> And spiraling upward to pierce the chink in the corner . . .
>
> For lately I think of my love for you and the rose
>   invading the darkness,
> And I long never to learn the difference.
>   ("The Rose Growing into the House")

You were walking alone
Down the slender almost-
Island of Catullus,
Walking the one green lane

Toward Desenzano,
In your arms the warm bread,
Olives, and the cool heady
Wine of Bardolino . . .

Not knowing I was only
Awaiting all my life,
You gave your one bay leaf
Away in Sirmione.

I hid it in my shade,
That slender book where late
This gesture of leaf-light
Touches your shoulder blade.
("Words to Accompany a Leaf from Sirmione")

The unhurried grace to be found in both these poems is carried in a clear conversational tone, never muffled and never importuning, intimate but not confessional, candid but not naked. These are poems of the steady voice and the level gaze; they are never unmanned by their passions because these poems have endured their passions for a long time.

In an interview with Wil Gehne published in the Winter 1989 issue of *Coraddi* Ruark spoke directly to the subject of clarity, distinguishing several varieties of the quality, and remarking that his preference is for "poems which are totally accessible on one level—all the way through—the first time you read them." In his qualifying phrase, "on one level," we may discover one of Ruark's strategic uses of clarity: a clear surface, by means of its attractive forward motion, can postpone a reader's expectations of profound or complicated thought until the more purely aesthetic design is seen and felt as a whole. Once the whole structure of a poem is perceived and reacted to on a powerful preliminary level, unhurried reflection reveals other levels and further implications; the total meaning of the poem becomes a delayed surprise. Now and again a practicing poet will hear from a member of his audience after he gives a public performance: "You know, I didn't understand what that poem was really about until I heard you read it." In the same way, the full force of some of Ruark's poems is likely to be known long after first acquaintance, and one's reaction is, "I didn't really understand that poem until now, but I never *misunderstood* it."

"Love Letter from Clarity in Chartres," following closely on the Sirmione poem in *Keeping Company,* uses the framework of a love poem addressed to the poet's wife to encompass several seemingly unrelated subjects, one of which is the effect of luminous clarity in art. Two friends have persuaded the speaker of the poem to depart Paris in order to visit Chartres cathedral. Because he is separated from his wife and thinking about her, he encounters a quality of light in the cathedral that reminds him of the light of her eyes.

> Now every arch is shocked with light around me,
>
> And I am standing in the sunlight of those years.
> Nothing but such clarity could say how clearly
> You shine to me through the blue silks of distance,
>
> Your rare and womanly friendliness,
> Your lovely sanity, your eyes as clear
> And delicate and less than everlasting
>
> As this sudden January light.

The similarity of the color of a woman's eyes and the light in the cathedral is not a metaphor many poets could have discovered, or, having discovered, would have pursued, but Ruark is not dismayed by its strangeness. In fact, this strangeness only leads him to a more daring trope, a comparison of the architecture of the cathedral with his wife's body, together with a contrast between the historied light of Europe and the fresh light of America, and another contrast between the immortality of art and the mortality of humanity.

Here in Chartres, this solitary sun,
Radiant as it is, seems to be wandering
Longingly after its own peculiar genius,

Thinking maybe to go down once in its too long life
Behind a remarkable hill in America,
The western slope of your own left shoulder,

Happy to light just briefly before it darkens
Forever your long articulate back
Whose brave architecture dreams

It will never sleep.

This long sentence, though complex in structure, seems so open in its meaning that we read it through to the end as a tender and wittily hyperbolic compliment to the loved one. When we examine it more closely, observing the different implications of "genius" and "remarkable" and "articulate" and discovering the syntactical ambiguities in the placement of "Forever" and of the whole final clause, other levels of meaning are unveiled, some of them quite plangent. Yet the poem remains a tender and witty love compliment. Its essential nature has not changed, but more of its nature has been revealed.

There are poems by John Crowe Ransom, Robert Lowell, Robert Frost, and many others, where close examination shows that the poem has a tendency counter to the one that a first reading comprehended, sometimes such a strong one that the poem can actually be read as saying the opposite of what even a perspicuous reader had supposed that it was saying. But there are other kinds of poems which do not use irony as a double-edged weapon, though it is possible that no written work ever escapes the umbrage of irony. Dante's sonnets, for example, unfold meanings continually upon rereading, but these meanings only amplify and qualify the poems as first perceived.

Ruark brings to this species of poem composed of innumerable lucid surfaces a special density of texture. Instead of employing a limited number of strands of imagery, metaphor, and incident, Ruark in his more ambitious poems applies a large palate of motif and through his unerring clarity of presentation keeps each motif forcefully individual even as it connects and intermingles with the others.

"Essay on Solitude" is a case in point. The poem begins with an allusion to one of Rilke's images for solitude—which it immediately pretends to replace; "I tell you he dreamed wrong."

> Human solitude is a slender single wing,
> The only thing born whole, undamaged, lovely,
> For all that flaring like a feathered wound.

The wing is not a completed object, as Rilke's "uncrumpled angel" is; it is, though "born whole," still "single."

The poem awakens from this dreamed image of solitude to morning sunlight, and the poet speaks of some of the unhappy careers of "heart-dark" solitaries he has known, and of their deaths by suicide. The deaths of his friends belong to the harsh sunlit world, and the poet and his wife retreat from this concept of reality that results in despair. He chooses as sigil for their life together a wood sorrel he had bought as a present for her one year ago, a plant that "folds its leaves / At the first sign of darkness, that opens them / Secretly as eyelids at first dawning." He identifies the two of them not with the starry blossoms of flowers but with the leaves which fold and unfold day and night always in the memoried presence of friends who are "folded up forever." The alar shape of the sorrel leaf reminds the poet of his wing image for solitude, and he imagines then the two leaf-wings, husband and wife, joined in a solitude that is both single and double, separate but joined—to make up, finally, the figure of Rilke's angel.

> Each is one leaf hovering near another
> Dreaming two leaves can fly out of darkness.
>
> Leaves fall out of light. Each solitude owns
> A simple death shawl dreaming in some darkness
> Its raveled hemline grazes the earth like a wing.
> It hurts to think between us we have a pair of them.

Ruark's poems resign themselves to a world in which struggle, disharmony, sorrow, and disaster are common, but never so common as to be unremarkable. His fourth volume, *Rescue the Perishing,*[4] takes violence as one of its themes; many of the poems in this book are set in Ireland and deal with civil strife. Ruark exhibits a deep and enduring love for this nation, but his most intense interests there are—characteristically—in nature and in literature. The pursuit of these gentle interests must take place against a background of revolutionary terror, and the poems are forced to remark upon the situation.

The violence is not something he desires to write about, as the divorcée publican in the barroom where he sits composing seems to know. He has shown this woman one of his love poems and she asks, "Don't you think love makes poetry possible?" Maybe it does, but on this rainy afternoon the poet happens to be working on a different kind of poem, one that reflects a different kind of experience:

> What can I say in Joe Nolan's quiet saloon,
> The rain-streaked window momentarily whole,
> About anything unshattered, poetry or love?
> I ask her the spelling of *gelignite.*
> She says it's no use in my peaceable poems.

These lines are from the second of two sonnets entitled "North Towards Armagh," and the irony implicit in the woman's fond rejoinder—that Ruark is not the sort of poet to deal with violent subjects—only underscores the more emphatic ironies of the sonnet he is engaged upon there, a poem called "Glasnevin" that speaks of a tourist pilgrimage "among the gravestones at Glasnevin, / Parnell, Maud Gonne MacBride, *diversi santi . . .*"

The following lines explicitly depict a contrasting violent scene:

> The Sten guns roared and adamant hymn singers
> Slumped in their bloody pews, and now, rung off
> This granite, the old staunch hymns are streaming
> From the country churches of my boyhood.

This bloody and tortured history cannot help changing the way we understand and react to Irish and English poetry. These are two of the most magnificent bodies of literature in the world, but even that magnificence must give way a little to the pressures of contemporary history, in the same way that the itinerary of the graveyard tour has been changed:

> With all the Republican dead so near,
> Our guide the begrudger, calling Hopkins
> "The convert," leads us first to the inventor
> Of plastic surgery, as well as he might,
> These days of the gelignite ascendancy.

First war; then, the grave of Gerard Manley Hopkins, with whom the guide seems impatient. Obviously, gelignite is very much in the ascendant, the civilized art of poetry in decline.

But the poet does not lose faith. *Rescue the Perishing* opens with "Postscript to an Elegy," a poem which reckons up the full burden of sorrow in losing a friend to violent death and speaks of the defenses which fail to keep the sorrow away: "Talk as I may of quickness and charm, easy laughter, / The forms of love, the sudden glint off silverware / At midnight will get in my eyes again." The elegy to which this poem is postscript is "For a Suicide, a Little Early Morning Music," which appears in *Keeping Company*. One of the reasons "Postscript" appears first in Ruark's fourth volume is to underline the continuation of the poet's concerns and the stability of his faith in the essentials of love, friendship, art, peace, nature, and poetry. The storms of circumstance shake him but do not destroy this faith.

Like "Postscript," "Leaving Hatteras" is companion to an earlier poem, discussed above. The death of the father, foreseen in "Night Fishing," has now taken place. The poet returns to the scene, the summertime coast of North Carolina. The details are not the same as before; for one thing, "Leaving Hatteras" is not a nocturne. But the locale is powerfully remindful: "The surf's invisible below the dunes, / But its sound is the fallback and lift of memory."

The poet remembers his father in a different way now—

not fishing in the undermining surf, but safe on the porch of a beach cabin. This time it is the boy who walks by the sea and in his reverie ("time forgetful of its calling") remembers the images with calm intensity:

> All I do is close my eyes. A screen door shudders
> And bangs and a boy lights out for the water
>
> And it is south of here by thirty years and more
> Where the shore curls inward and the dunes are lower
> And a boy can see his father from the water
> Cleaning and oiling his tackle in a porch chair.

"Leaving Hatteras" is one of Ruark's most adroit accomplishments, and all the more adroit in being so accomplished that its skillfulness is made almost invisible. The whole poem is suffused with heat, drowse, hypnotic surf-murmur, subtle but palpable presence of memory, memory in reverie become so actualized that when the speaker and his brother stand ready to depart, the father is with them in the cabin:

> Here what looks like water shivers over the screens
>
> And we breathe deep, two of us only, buttoning
> Our sleeves and zipping up the nylon duffel bags,
> Unless you count the lazybones in the doorway,
> Stretching himself and rubbing his eyes with his knuckles,
> Blinking like a child as the room turns familiar.

Any future estimate of Ruark's work will have to take careful account of his continual return to favored themes, of the ways in which the earlier poems and the later hold converse together, their motifs deepening and mellowing, the strange becoming familiar and the familiar turning strange again.

The turmoils of our present predicament must be faced but must not be allowed to triumph: in the poetry of Gibbons Ruark the only final catastrophe would be oblivious forgetfulness. He beautifully avers a faith that calmness and steadiness of vision, constancy and wholeness of love, can achieve a peace that forms the center of the personality. In hours of serenity, as well as in hours of conflict, the necessity for courage is a pressing one, but there are examples to live by, words to cherish—like the last words and the *fact* of the last words of Mozart, as Ruark recalls them in his elegy for James Wright in *Keeping Company*, where the composer, "breathing his last music," still manages

> Somehow to say in time, "And now I must go,
> When I have only just learned to live quietly."

NOTES

1. *Keeping Company* (Baltimore: Johns Hopkins University Press, 1983).
2. *A Program for Survival* (Charlottesville: University Press of Virginia, 1971).
3. *Reeds* (Lubbock: Texas Tech University Press, 1978).
4. *Rescue the Perishing* (Baton Rouge: Louisiana State University Press, 1991).

The Poet and the Plowman

Surprisingly often we talked about Vergil, usually about the *Aeneid,* but sometimes about the *Georgics,* and then with the wry sentimental fondness of old students who had been made, not quite willingly, to go to school to the poem. And during the plentiful longueurs of the Redskins games of the mid-1960s, we would regret that so many traditional attractions of farm life had seemed to disappear along with our Latin. Then he would smile and say in his breathy ironic genteel Kentucky accent: "But we would make dreadful farmers, Fred, you and I."

This was Allen Tate, who would spend Sunday afternoons at my home during his two-week teaching stints in Greensboro at the local University of North Carolina because I enjoyed watching television football with him. ("I admire the precision," he said. "Machine-like.") He maintained that poets should be only spectator farmers—doubting that Vergil had ever struck a lick with a hoe—and that when they became active husbandmen, they cut ridiculous figures or were unhappy and embittered. He was thinking of Jesse Stuart and Robert Frost and of Hesiod, and I thought of the bittersweet work of Wendell Berry.

It was partly because of his allegiance to the values of an agricultural society that he liked to describe himself as a "reactionary." That was rather a belligerent term in the 1960s (and must have been more so in the 1930s when he developed his stance), and I was puzzled by it. Later I came to understand

---

From *Chronicles* 10, no. 7 (July 1986).

that for Mr. Tate, it meant something like "radical conservative," and that he was pleased to align himself with Poe and John C. Calhoun equally. The more thoughtful attitudes are the harder to define, and his usage of "reactionary" was both ironic and earnest at the same time.

The ageless relationship between poetry and farming has always been sentimental and ironic; the two disciplines would seem to have mostly accidental requirements in common: patience, fatalism, renunciation, awe of nature, reverence for the earth. When we remind ourselves that our word *verse* came originally from *versus,* turning the plow at the end of a furrow, we must wonder what strange terrain the contemporary poet is tilling with his wildly staggered furrows. When we think of the small farmer supporting his agriculture by means of another job in factory or town, perhaps we think of all the American poets perched at insecure university posts. Othello's occupation is not gone, not in our century; but Cincinnatus's is—and maybe Vergil's also.

It has never been possible to say where the poet fits in the basic economies of nations, but it has always been clear that the farmer lodges at the bottom, as the necessary and unchangeable foundation. The position may be necessary, but it is not glamorous. Scholars have faithfully diminished the old legend about the *Georgics,* that the poem was written at the suggestion of Augustus in order to lure farmer-soldiers back to the land after they had acquired a taste for plunder, luxury, and urbanity. ("How you gonna keep 'em down on the farm after they've seen Paree?") But the legend did account for the double nature of the poem which, while it celebrates the grandeur of the land and hieratic ceremoniousness of farm work, does not stint in pointing out the difficulties and dangers. The poet is careful to draw in the disasters of flood, fire, drought, frost, and crop failure; whoever they were, his intended audience was not naive.

On one side, then, the poem is acceptably realistic, but Vergil is also at pains to show that he stands at some distance from his subject, that his poem is a bookish poem. He pays direct tribute to some of his sources; Aristaeus, Hesiod, Cato the Elder, Aristotle. If the celebratory aspect of the poem is always brightened by a deliberate and artificial appeal to the myth of the Golden Age, the didactic passages are carefully informed by the best scientific knowledge of the time.

But that may have been a necessary mistake. Nothing quaintifies so quickly as scientific knowledge, and our century, which had deceived itself into believing that it actually knows something about nature, may look upon the *Georgics* as no more than a curious compilation of ancient error. There are, for example, the long famous passages about bee society in which Vergil describes the control of the hive under the King Bee and gives an account of the spontaneous generation of the insect. My own copy of the *Georgics* is an 1816 reprint on the 1740 edition by John Martyn, then professor of botany at Cambridge, who differs from our contemporary scientists in his anxiety to vindicate Vergil rather than to refute him. When he must correct rather than support the information, he displays a pleasing diffidence: "The Poet's account of the generation of bees is by no means consistent with the doctrine of the modern philosophers, who assert with great probablity, that no animal, or even plant, is produced without a concurrence of the two sexes. However, the doctrine of equivocal generation was so generally admitted by the ancients that it is no wonder the Poet should assent to it." (Martyn's phrase, "or even plant," probably indicates that he has but lately accepted the ideas of Linnaeus.) And on the matter of the King: "But the modern philosophers have been more happy in discovering the nature of these wonderful insects. The labouring bees do not appear to be of either sex; the drones are discovered to have the male organs of generation; and the king is found to be of the female sex."

But our twentieth-century scientists love pecking orders; they have arranged an inflexible one among their own disciplines, with particle physics at the top and sociology or maybe economics at the bottom. If they were asked to rank the poet as a purveyor of reliable knowledge, they might place him somewhere below a computer software salesman and only slightly above a political candidate. It was this sort of arrogance that rankled John Crowe Ransom and Allen Tate, and they took up arms to defend poetry against it. Mr. Tate was very proud of Ransom's definition of poetry as *knowledge car-*

ried to the heart, and on the several occasions when he quoted it to me, he underlined it with a significant glance.

That is a nifty and telling phrase, but it does not answer all objections. Can every sort of knowledge be fashioned into poetry and given such memorable emotional force that it is carried to the heart? T. S. Eliot denied the possibility of a modern counterpart to the *Georgics,* declaring informational didactic poetry dead as a form. But Eliot's dictum probably points up a fact the contemporary poet does not like to admit: that for all its vaunted toughness, modern poetry simply cannot accommodate such masses of obvious and irreplaceable information as we find in Vergil's lines. Even the current preoccupation with brutality and despair is only a symptom of preciosity. A poetry which can no longer rejoice in daily homely labor, which cannot—in Vergil's phrase—honor the plow, will never be convincing in its continual wheedling about political injustice.

Nudus ara, sere nudus. "Plow naked, naked sow," Vergil tells us. The scientist will surely find this bit of advice characteristically silly, but the elder farmers I remember from my youth would know instinctively what it means—and Vance Randolph reports the practice carried out to the letter in remote spots in Arkansas even in the 1930s. The words are there to remind us of the ceremonial, and ultimately religious, nature of farming; they remind us of the selfless rituals we must undergo in order to keep faith.

On the subject of this faith I could never do better than to quote John S. Collis on the potato:

> When we eat a potato we eat the earth, and we eat the sky. It is the law of nature that all things are all things. That which does not appear to exist to-day is to-morrow hewn down and cast into the oven. Nature carries on by taking in her own washing. That is Nature's economy, contrary to political economy; so that he who cries "Wolf! Wolf!" is numbered amongst the infidels. . . . What is an infidel? One who lacks faith. What creates faith? A miracle. How then can there be a faithless man found in the world? Because many men have cut off the nervous communication between the eye and the brain. In the madness of blindness they are at the mercy of intellectual nay-sayers,

theorists, theologians, and other enemies of God. But it doesn't matter; in spite of them, faith is reborn when anyone chooses to take a good look at anything—even a potato.

This passage is from Collis's *The Worm Forgives the Plough;* his best book, *While Following the Plough,* is perhaps also the best—though unintended—commentary on the *Georgics.* It has been out of print for exactly forty-six years.

But the question becomes, would our poets understand Vergil's advice to plow and sow naked? The largest purpose of the *Georgics* is not to dignify, but to sanctify, honest farm labor. A reader who has not looked at it in a long time finds he has forgotten that the poem is full of stars. Even the smallest task must be undertaken in due season under the proper constellations. These prescriptions are not mere meteorology; they connect the order of the earth to the order of the stars. The farmer moves by the motion of the stars, and his labors determine the concerns of the government. The Roman State is not founded upon the soil, it is founded in the universe. And so were all the other civilizations which managed to endure for any length of time. If poets do not wish to study these matters and treat of them, they shirk their responsibilities and fail their society.

Yet I suppose that if a contemporary poet does not feel this responsibility, then it is not his. It is all too easy to sit in a self-appointed judgment seat and allocate responsibilities to one's fellows. The impulse to do so may even proceed from Vergil, who had a very acute sense of responsibility. The *Georgics* and the *Aeneid* were his duties rather than his pleasure. An honorable tradition makes poetry secondary in his affections; he had more love of philosophy, and the passage of the second Georgic in which he speaks of his Lucretian ambitions is truly poignant:

And may the lovely Muses first of all
(Whose priest I am, love-struck by poetry)
Accept me; show me the roads of heaven, the stars,
The various solar eclipses, works of the moon,
Earthquakes, what forces make the high seas

Swell and ruin the shores and once again
Fall back, and why the suns of winter hasten
To dive into the ocean, or what delay
Obstructs the winter nights that move so slowly.
But if my heart's own cooling blood prevents
Attaining to these properties of nature,
Let me love the fields and valley streams,
The unassuming woods and rivers. The meadows,
Sperchius, Taygetus where the Spartan virgins
Dance: there, or in the cool vale under Haemus,
Let someone place me in broad shade of branches.
That man was happy who could know the causes
Of things and under his feet could trample fear,
Unyielding fate, and the roar of greedy Acheron.

And there is a sense in which he has overfulfilled his responsibilities. It is credible from our perspective to find the largest fault of his rural poem in its enormous influence. The *Georgics* is the wishful cornerstone of the Jeffersonian utopia, a nation of small landholders. If the poem contains enough realistic detail to be convincing, it is still a fairy tale at heart. There is no mention of slave labor in the *Georgics,* nor even of hired labor. The farmer is enjoined to be content with a modest farm that will just support his family. But three bad years in a row, or precipitous debtorship, will make beggars of this family. We read now with special sadness the lines in which security is named as the chief comfort of the farmer's life:

The farmer divides the earth with crooked plow;
This the year's whole labor: thus he sustains
His little family and his fatherland,
His herd of cows and his blue ribbon bulls.

"Perhaps it may still be possible," we think, forgetting that Vergil places this idyllic picture in the mythic past, under the reign of aureus Saturnus, golden Saturn, before iron Jupiter seized the scepter.

Probably the poet was never the substantial friend the farmer was looking for. Still he has proved a better friend than the scientist and the government expert. He has generally shown admiration rather than contempt for the farmer's personal capacities, and if his advice has not always been useful, at least it has not been deadly.

Mr. Tate was right, of course. Most poets would make better lutenists than farmers. But even the most inept of us still feel close kinship with the man in the fields, with his life of ordered observation and inspired patience. That is the one life besides poetry and natural philosophy that still touches an essential harmony of things, and when a civilization discards that way of life, it breaks the most fundamental covenant mankind can remember.

Chronicling the Culture

The Poet and the Modern Epic Ambition

A culture chronicles itself. The archeologist, the anthropologist and the sociologist, the novelist and his brethren in stagecraft and filmcraft, all lead us to appreciate that we live in an ocean of documentary material. The look of our automobiles, the diction of our news reporting, the images of our television advertising, the cut of our clothing, the texture of our mathematics—all these things and a million others provide indices to the collective characters of each of our national cultures and to the character of our global culture, if we can truly be said to have achieved one.

Not only are the professions I have already listed taking on the job of dealing with this infinite clutter of information and implication, but other professions are equally interested, and are engaged in examining each possible trend and countertrend, each minuscule revolution and consequent revision, from different perspectives in pursuit of different goals.

We might mention, for example, the historian and the news reporter, the market research analyst and the advertising copy writer, the government census bureaucrat and the public works engineer—each of these professions and a thousand others have a stake in looking at the morass of clues before them and then trying to determine the outlines of our contemporary personalities, individual as well as collective. All sorts of

---

From *Imprimis* 18, no. 5 (May 1989); reprinted in *The Formalist* 1, no. 2 (1990).

methods have been devised to undertake the smaller separate tasks that the larger task entails; the most pervasive method is quantification, the reducing of historical facts and conscious thought and idiosyncratic impulse to processable numbers.

The Poet as a Chronicler

And there is the pinch, so far as the poet is concerned. For the poet too is highly motivated to analyze and understand and finally to synthesize all the various cultural data that he can come by while still retaining his identity as a poet. Yet the poet is no quantifier—except in the metric quantities of his lines. The methods the poet has at his disposal—intuitive understanding of character, wide knowledge of history, close observation of nature and of psychology, a highly sensitive patterning of his autobiography, and so forth—are not considered trustworthy in any scientific sense. The quality which gives his work its singular and enduring value is its brave subjectivity, a quality which at the present moment is rejected as unscientific, irrelevant, and unimportant.

But "relevance" and "importance" are transitory qualities as well as relative ones. In 1929 it was a matter of some expense as well as of dogged labor to find out just how many tons of pig iron were produced in the United States and how many bushels of sweet potatoes were consumed, how many hospitals were erected and how many tenements were demolished, and it seemed important to know these facts. These are facts which no doubt still have their uses for economic historians, for statistical forecasters, and for a few other professionals. For almost all of us, though, they are now more remote in interest than the minutest subatomic particle or the farthest astronomical object. They sleep the sleep of disused filing cabinets.

The Poet as a Muse

Now, of course, it is the responsibility of literature to be interesting. No one talks about it much, but it is the first duty of poetry to entertain. After that, it can instruct, enlighten, ennoble, and perform all the high-minded feats of intellectual and moral gymnastics that it ever has a yearning to perform. But first it must flag our attentions and then engage our emotions in a way that 740,000 cubic tons of pig iron and the nearly twelve million bushels of sweet potatoes do not.

I am perfectly aware that Hart Crane's impressionistic American epic poem, *The Bridge,* does not flag the attentions and capture the emotions of everyone who reads it—and that it hasn't acquired milling hordes of faithful readers in the first place. I know that there are many people for whom a phrase like "O Thou Hand of Fire" is less thrilling than "O Thou Pan of Pizza," for whom a line like "The seal's wide spindrift gaze toward paradise" has one thousand times less meaning than a weary cliché from rock and roll lyrics: "Come on, baby, it's all right!"

Nevertheless, there are certain readers for whom *The Bridge* is an entertaining performance, and it is to these readers that poets must address themselves, partly because they must find their audiences where they can, and partly because American culture, for all its self-vaunting anti-intellectualism, still does not consist entirely in pizza and rock and roll. Poetry, and especially epic poetry, is supposed to be a more durable stuff than pizza; whether it can ever be as entertaining is a doubtful point.

The Poet as a Prophet

But an epic poem is an enduring object because its subject matter is enduring, its subject matter being in the long run the very culture that demanded—or caused, or evolved—its production. Once we think that Vergil's purpose in the *Aeneid* was not only to tell the story of the founding of Rome, but also to draw the lineaments of Roman ideals as they will always be perceived in history; once we see that Milton's purpose in *Paradise Lost* is not simply to recast the Biblical compilation into Hellenic epic form, but to dramatize at the highest ontological and cosmological levels the eternal dialectic between rebellion and authority, between necessary error and merciful justice; then we see the magnitude of the effort that lies before the poet. He must find the form, the story, and the poetic idiom that will eternalize these conflicts and concerns that underlie and animate his own time, even if these conflicts and concerns are generally unrecognized in his generation. The poet's ambitions in regard to his culture are different from those of the politician on one side and of the historian on the other.

The Poet as a Judge

The politician wishes to understand his culture; at least, the bright and farseeing politician does. But his goals are immediate. He wants to understand his culture so that he can effect immediate change, sometimes violent change. He wants to lay hands on his society and culture and to leave the impress of his personality upon the daily lives of his fellow citizens. The historian's ambitions may be greater than the politician's in some respects, but they are less immediate. Ideally, the historian of the contemporary world wishes to comprehend his times without effecting immediate change. He may celebrate what he finds good and denigrate what he considers bad; he may acclaim with wholehearted approval or he may view with alarm. If he refuses to judge character, circumstance, and event, then he is no historian but only a glorified statistician. But he is powerless to enforce his judgments. Once he attempts to enforce his judgments, then he reduces himself to a politician—or to a soldier, who in historic terms is merely the instrument of political policy. In order to achieve what objectivity he can, he must stand back from participation and disengage himself from the activities that inevitably result in partisan bias.

(I am speaking, of course, in generalized ideal terms. The politician can sometimes be a perspicacious historian and even a perspicuous philosopher—as Cicero was. Or the most hotly engaged participant in historical affairs can prove himself an immortal historian—as Julius Caesar has done.)

Somewhere between these two positions, the politician as busy meddler and the historian as ivory tower voyeur, lie the activities of most professions whose business consists in the direct observation of culture. The government bureaucratic information-gatherer does not ordinarily directly affect current events, but he supplies information to those individuals who are in position to do so. The literary critic is not a direct influence; that is, he does not cause this book to be written and that other one to languish unpublished; but his suggestions that one author rewards the time and effort required to read him while another author is an abyss of murkiest idiocy exert a strong indirect influence on the temporary intellectual complexion of his time. Sooner or later it is discovered that the bureaucrat's statistics were faulty or irrelevant and that the literary critic's judgments were dead wrong from top to bottom, but that outcome is what makes these professionals historical personages rather than historians. Most professions which deal with culture—journalism, teaching, sociology, advertising, and so forth—occupy this middle ground between direct action and self-sufficient contemplation.

But the ambitions of the poet seem different and quite apart from those of the other workers in his subject matter. He has no hope (except in his capacities as a private citizen, as a soldier or as a voter, or in other civic responsibilities) of directly affecting current events or of changing the face of his contemporary culture. If he is wise, he has no desire to do these things, for the poet is ill equipped to be a public leader.

The Poet as a Man

It has long been a demonstrable fact that the poet as personality is a cranky, off-putting pain in the butt. Bumptious, bilious, and babbling; irresponsible, irreal, and well irrigated; lewd, loudmouthed, and lunatic, he does not present an edifying spectacle to the society that he must portray for the delectation of succeeding generations. The figure of the poet has been delineated for us in the literature of the millenia, and he makes an all-too-human design upon this literature, ranging the gamut from the true picture of bravery and nobility with Sir Philip Sidney to the true picture of funkiness and petty outlawry with François Villon.

Between these contrasting examples we find the usual picture of the poet as a nearsighted scribe and harmless drudge who has been made absent-minded and just a little daft by his books and his dreams, by his flagons and apples, by his inattentive lightminded girlfriends. There he is, as in the opera *The Tales of Hoffman,* tipsy and humiliated at the beginning, drunk and insensible to the revelations of his own muse at the end.

Even if that rendering of the poet is a caricature, we must recognize that the poet is almost certainly not the pilot we wish to find at the helm of state. When we try to place the poet within the context of Horace's metaphor of the ship of state, the image that inevitably comes to mind is that of the loose cannon on deck. Politics demands passion, but disciplined passion; for the poet, discipline is the business of writing, passion the business of life.

The Poet as a Teller of Truths

No, that formulation is not true. For if the poet should not aspire to the role of politician, neither should he aspire to the role of historian. Those dry, discarded, dull statistics that I have been speaking of with such cavalier superciliousness are daily meat and drink to the conscientious historian. They are not the whole of the raw material that he makes history of; sometimes they are barely ancillary to his purposes. But he must know them and respect them if his work is to have basis in truth and a claim upon comprehensiveness.

The poet must know *about* the pig iron and sweet potato statistics, and he will aid his epic poem by knowing where to find such information, but he is not constrained to absorb these facts into his work. He is not even constrained to honor them.

If the dramatic exigencies of his poem require that in 1929 the United States produced only thirty-five pounds of pig iron rather than 740,000 cubic tons, then he must write down thirty-five pounds. If his poem demands no sweet potatoes, then it must go yamless, and to hell with those numbers collected so expensively and assiduously. The poet displays an attitude toward raw fact that would give a real historian apoplexy.

But if he is not going to tell us the truth about sweet potatoes and pig iron, then the poet had better substitute some value that we can recognize as being larger and more important than factual accuracy. Aristotle believed that he knew what this value was; he called it "truth," poetic truth in strong distinction to mere accuracy. The truth the poet creates, or discovers, is the general grand design that underlies the infinity of quotidian detail. The historian arranges his data into a narrative; the poet shapes a narrative into a plot. However complex his plot appears to us, it is still quite simple when compared to the complexities of his raw material. His story is to be simple, striking, unforgettable, judicious, convincing; and what it lacks in strict historical accuracy it must make up in excitement. If he can portray strong characters who perform brave actions out of comprehensible motives, then he shall command our warmest allegiances. If he must resort to other means in order to create excitement, we shall probably still look upon his work with interest, but we shall have—reservations.

About our modern attempts at epic poems, we have misgivings. In the twentieth-century English language epic poem, the broadly persuasive, emotionally satisfying plot has disappeared, and the heroes who might animate it have decamped. When we look at the works of Ezra Pound, Basil Bunting, T. S. Eliot, Michael Martin, Louis Zukofsky, Amon Liner, William Carlos Williams, Charles Olson, William Harmon, Ronald Johnson, Hart Crane, Ron Bayes, and others, we find that the epic poem (and also the longish poems which make no claims on epic status) has been redefined so that our usual expectations must be disappointed. And just as the form has been redefined, the methods of composition have been transformed; sometimes, in fact, the compositional methods have been turned upside down.

Some of the larger questions that the epic form broaches have been retained and two of them have been made the main points of these poets' concern. The first question is: *What is the relationship of culture to the individual life in our contemporary world?* The second question is: *What constant qualities of history, if any, are exemplified or illustrated by our isolated modern biographies?*

These are traditional questions. If we examine the latter question first, the problem of the relationship of epic characters to the lessons of history, we can point out that *pius* Aeneas, for example, embodies the primary bond of relationship between the individual Roman citizen and the Roman state; it is duty. We can see that Dante's epic hero is a historical constant; the poet himself stands as Everyman in his search for the correct relationship with God. As for the first question about the relationship of culture to individual life, all the epic heroes illustrate the same standard proper role: The individual acts in accordance with the highest ideals of his society. In doing so, he gives them living reality, flesh and blood incarnation, and in the act of obeying them raises these same ideals to even higher levels. The hero's physical bravery is only a part of the quality of character his role demands; he must also make difficult moral choices. Achilles must kill Hector, even though his feelings make this final act distasteful; Aeneas must desert Dido, even though his betrayal makes him for the moment an arrant villain; Dante must show no pity for the tortures of his friends and acquaintances because the pains they endure are only those that their sins have led them to deserve. Some circumstances demand that the epic hero be hardheaded, other circumstances make him seem to be hardhearted, but he follows a code that justifies his behavior; it is a comprehensible code that is provided for him by the culture which he inhabits, and in following the dictates of this code he preserves the culture which produced it. The relationship of the epic hero to his culture becomes at climactic moments a one-to-one relationship; the culture creates the man, the man preserves the culture; they are one and the same, policy and instrument, concept and embodiment, absorbed into a single figure. The relationship is not merely comprehensible, it comes to seem inevitable. It makes a very neat package.

The Contemporary Epic Poem

With the twentieth century, though, we come to a time when the neat package is suspect. Whether the modern poet is right or wrong in his judgment, he has rejected the traditional form and some of the traditional goals and methods of the epic poem as we receive the form from Homer and Vergil, from Statius and Milton. The poet feels that this our modern age requires a different sort of object, a variation upon the ancient form.

For the sake of clarity I will oversimplify the modern poet's position. He wakes up one morning and says to himself, or to the world at large: "This is a lovely Tuesday morning and my time is free until noon. Just the day to embark upon an epic. I want my poem to reflect the temper of my own time and to preserve the lineaments of my culture for generations to come, but also to display a historically necessary tie to earlier times, to the centuries that fell before me. Yet when I look out my study window upon the world that I must live in, all I see are disaster, formlessness, motion without purpose, rampant accidents, confusion twice confounded, perplexity doubly perplexed. It seems to me that this confusion, this impression of sheer randomness that I find in modern life, ought to be embodied in my epic if my work is to be truthful. If my poem is to possess validity and integrity, if it is to be an accurate speculum of its milieu, then it must present to its audience a fragmented aspect, a jumbled jigsaw-puzzle appearance."

There is a certain logic in this notion, though it may be a specious logic. After all, a confused and confusing poem is not too difficult to achieve. Many of us set down one almost every week while trying to write a poem that is clear, whole, and seamless, and it is vexing to think that another writer may receive wide acclaim for accomplishing what we less fortunate mortals have labored so earnestly to avoid.

Yet our modern epic poet may have a cannier purpose in

mind than we have surmised. "I'm not *really* crazy," he shall tell us, "nor is my poem. It has a secret structure that is hidden by its bewildering surface." Then he proceeds to point out to us arcane principles of structure, unnoticed axioms of organization, subterranean networks of relationships, correspondences, and associations. And so it turns out that this object which has appeared to be so haphazard and patchwork can actually be clarified with a diagram. Aren't we all now reassured of the poet's sanity?

Perhaps we are. Perhaps not. For it is a wild connect-the-dots scheme, this construction of the contemporary epic. The countless separate facts and artifacts of our culture glow in the poet's range of vision like the points of light in a star-field photograph, and the poet is to draw lines of significant connection between a comparative few of them until he has discovered a new constellation among these stars, or has imposed one of his own devising upon them. The poet likes to think that he has discovered connections, while we his readers can only believe that he has imposed an order, an arbitrary and ramshackle sort of organization. Still he gets the benefit of the doubt because we recognize the magnitude and difficulty of his undertaking and because even an inchoate or intimated idea of purpose is better than none at all. The surface, however, can be very confusing indeed.

Ezra Pound was at pains to redefine the epic in his famous *Cantos*. He chucked out the notion of plot, insisted upon different qualities of character and purpose for his multi-personed hero, and made demotic heightened diction of the epic idiom. His reformulation of the epic was simplicity itself: "The epic is a long poem containing history." And he believed that his *Cantos* fulfilled this single requirement.

Probably he was wrong. It is too easy to argue that the narrative of *The Cantos*, insofar as it can be discerned, lacks the dignity and consistency of a plot, that its tatterdemalion design prevents the poem from containing anything, much less history. Pound's *Cantos* point toward history but do not contain it, in the same way that the Goodwill shop and the want ads of the newspaper tell us something about our culture without adding up to coherent commentary.

And what we say of *The Cantos,* we can with equal justice say of Williams's *Paterson,* of Olson's Maximus poems, of Zukofsky's *A,* and of *The Bridge.* We can even make the same criticism of *The Waste Land,* though we would have to soften our stricture by pointing out that Eliot's incoherence is a necessary part of his purpose.

From Randomness to Meaning

The traditional epic form took the historian's narrative and shaped it into the simple grand architecture of a plot; the modern epic takes the historian's narrative and, in a spirit of heated distrust, pulverizes it into a dust of separate and discrete moments, a rubble of footnotes. The traditional epic starts in the middle of its story, moves to the beginning, and finishes at the end. The modern epic begins anywhere and finishes when the poet leaves off writing. Whatever the subject matter of the modern epic, and whatever the ostensible and announced themes, three secondary themes will inevitably be articulated because of the poet's choice of structure. Whether it does so consciously or not, the modern epic poem will deal with disintegration, disconnection, and loneliness.

It will deal with these subjects because these are the terms in which the modern poet sees history. The prevalence of these terms might indicate that our modern age has acquired a healthy skepticism about the past, that it refuses to whitewash, romanticize, or ameliorate the harsh facts that undoubtedly obtained in the past. I'm sure that we would like to believe that we are less deceived than our forefathers. That is a harmless enough vanity, isn't it? Maybe it's not so harmless. Perhaps we ought to name this notion the Monty Python School of Historiography, the one that avers that if people in the Middle Ages smelled bad, then it must have been impossible for them to think clearly or to live nobly. Professor Dan Sundahl of Hillsdale College has pointed toward the lack of a historical sensibility as resulting for modern poets in a lack of "viable poetic stuff." "Fully to appreciate the grandeur of the epic might therefore mean that the persons whose lives are too special fail to read and understand history as meta-history—so to speak." I take Dr. Sundahl's meaning here as the idea that the poet, having become a specialist in isolated historical detail, has lost his sense of community with the people of the past and no longer knows them as people, but as examples or as tendencies or symptoms of larger trends of history. Dr. Sundahl continues: "It has always seemed to me that the epic somehow inverts itself so that eternity somehow leaks into the poet's own time."

The good professor's cautious double use of "somehow" reveals that he is aware that his suggestion about the relationship of the epic to time verges upon the mystical. But in order to appreciate the spirit of the epic, in order to enter into a knowledgeable relationship with its purposes, we must put aside some small part of our rational skepticism. We are forced to accept the exaggerations of the poet as being more appropriate to his history as well as to his artistry than a more seemingly accurate account would be. The fables that the poet asks us to accept are no more far-fetched than many of the things that contemporary physical science asks us to believe, especially if we are reading in quantum theory or superstring theory.

Did a historical personage named Aeneas actually carry his father on his back out of the wrack of burning Troy? If I can be convinced that it is statistically necessary for an electron to be in two different places at the same time, then I may as well believe the story of Aeneas, and I shall understand Vergil's purposes better if I do believe his story than if I do not.

To this degree I share in the mystical attitude toward the epic. While I am engaged with Homer's plot, I shall subscribe to the details he gives me because in that way his vision is understood to be whole and unqualified. When I close *The Iliad* and turn my attention to other matters, then I can pick and choose what to believe and disbelieve about the poem and within the poem. But if I have not faith in the poem while I read it, I have missed its experience.

Homer's experience was not different in degree of difficulty from yours and mine. The world presented itself to him as a confusing mass of fragments, as a warehouse of disconnected parts, as a whisper-gallery of rumors. But he had faith that in fashioning a plot from all the random matter, he would find meaning, and a truth that would have value. I like to think that he believed his work would endure. We know that Milton had that faith.

But lately we have lost it. The factual accuracy about the separate details has come to triumph over the sense of design, and we believe that these two requirements are in opposition to one another.

And to a certain extent they are, but not entirely. When the epic poem about George Washington is written at last, it will not contain the story of the cherry tree. But it will tell us, using the materials that we already know almost by heart, a story that we have never heard before, a story large, majestic, and truthful, even though the ledger numbers about pig iron and sweet potatoes shall have been juggled in a manner so graceful as to be almost unnoticeable.

The Man Who Named the McPoem

It was Donald Hall who gave us that useful and precise critical term "McPoem" to describe the garden variety contemporary effort in flabby free verse whose dismal ambitions are set to a wheezy music. Hall is a savvy and perspicacious critic and the bloke who undertakes to write about his work has the immediate task of not appearing a fool before his subject.

But with the best intentions in the world, the best preparation and the most meticulous care, we all write a certain number of McPoems. I've done so. So have Robert Penn Warren and Howard Nemerov and Richard Wilbur. Donald Hall has published more than a few, as he will sorrowfully admit. In fact, it was he and Robert Bly and Louis Simpson and Galway Kinnell who helped to develop the McPoem in the 1960s by borrowing surrealism's quaintest mannerisms. This stuff was called Deep Image poetry and constituted a sort of versified Method Acting mumble. Here is a sample from Hall's "The Alligator Bride":

> The sky is a gun aimed at me.
> I pull the trigger.
> The skull of my promises
> leans in a black closet, gapes
> with its good mouth
> for a teat to suck.

From *Chronicles* 15, no. 2 (February 1991). A review of *Old and New Poems,* by Donald Hall.

In about three days college sophomores learned to write this kind of yammer by the yard; in another week they learned to think it was poetry.

If Donald Hall felt called upon to defend these lines, he would make a good case for them; in literature everything is defensible because everything is open to attack, and Hall's best critical work is his appreciations of other poets. The silly passage above may be justified by autobiographical circumstance: several times in his career Hall has foundered, has fallen into dry spells and halted verse composition entirely. Then he found a way to begin anew, writing in a style that looks radically different from what came before. "The Alligator Bride" is one of a number of poems that enabled Hall to pick up his pen and start over. Other poems that mark similar stages are "The Long River," "The Blue Wing," and "Kicking the Leaves."

The broad variety of Hall's writing has long been a source of wonder. Besides poetry and criticism, he has published fiction, drama, children's literature, biography, and reminiscence. His poetry encompasses all sorts of forms, from steely epigrams, like the one addressed to a philosopher ("The world is everything that is the case. / Now stop your blubbering and wash your face"), to an attempt at a contemporary epic. This latter poem, called *The One Day,* is an honorable attempt, but hobbled by muddy organization and some puffy rhetoric. It won an award from the National Book Critics Circle, a group whose selection committees have boasted in the organization's newsletter that they don't like poetry and don't read it.

But it is not Hall's fault that a horde of critical midges have conspired to give him a prize for work that is not his best. His best work is very fine indeed and there is plenty of it. So much of it, in fact, that my list of favorite poems is too long to include here. But I will name a few I consider among the best written in two generations: "Exile," "At Delphi," "The Long River," "The Moon," "Beau of the Dead," "In the Kitchen of the Old House," "The Blue Wing," "The Table," "Kicking the Leaves," "The Black-Faced Sheep," "Names of Horses," "Whip-Poor-Will," "Old Timers' Day," and "On a Horse Carved in Wood."

Knowing readers will see that I've included a few Deep Image poems among my tiptop favorites. When Donald Hall is writing well, he can bring to almost any kind of discourse a profound and polished wit, a fineness of observation that a naturalist might envy, and a warm and ready affection. These qualities are controlled by a firm intelligence, a sly curiosity, and a wary critical sense.

When he makes mistakes it is sometimes because he tries to write beyond his means. One of his character traits is an admiration of the vatic voice, the mystic vision; he would like to achieve some of the effects we find in James Wright and Robert Bly, or even in William Blake and Walt Whitman. It is probably Whitman who tempts him into such lugubrious mistakes as these lines from "Praise for Death": "Let us praise death in old age. Wagging our tails, / bowing, whimpering, let us praise sudden crib-death / and death in battle." It was the thought of Whitman or of Christopher Smart that caused him to write: "We praise death when we smoke, and when we stop smoking."

But if these aberrant lines are set against the last stanza of "At Delphi" we see the difference when the poet is at the top of his form. Before knowing this poem, I could never imagine that I would find an American lyric that would give me the sensation of being a figure in a painting by Hubert Robert or Claude Lorrain. The speaker of "At Delphi" has told of a visit to the city of the ancient oracle and of his remembering the history of the locale. These final lines distill his experience:

> No priestess spoke. I heard one sound.
> The donkey's sure and nerveless plod
> Past ruined columns of a god
>   Made dactyls on the ground.

I am not merely praising the restraint of the lines, though Hall knows well an important point of which others are unaware—that restraint is not a negative virtue. It is just that in these lines a quiet tone sounds a deeper resonance than in other poems where the voice straining for prophecy drowns out nuance.

When Hall's ebullience is successful, though, he is more effective than Allen Ginsburg or Anne Waldman or Diane Wakoski or two score other poets who have made careers of ranting. One poem, "O Cheese," is intended partly as a send-up of the relentless apostrophizers. ("O cheeses of gravity, cheeses of wistfulness, cheeses that weep continually because they know they will die.") When his considerable and considered humor animates his phrases, we can often find lines as charming as this description of cows in "Great Day in the Cows' House":

> Now these wallowing
> big-eyed calf-makers, bone-rafters for leather,
> awkward arks, cud-chewing lethargic mooers,
> roll their enormous heads, trot, gallop, bounce,
> cavort, stretch, leap, and bellow—
> as if everything heavy and cold vanished at once
> and cow spirits floated
> weightless as clouds in the great day's windy April.

But for Hall the road of excess does not always lead to the palace of wisdom. His humor too may betray him and in a prose poem called "The Presidentiad" it does so murderously. I will quote two sentences simply to show that *aliquando dormitat bonus Homerus,* that even the brightest among us may have profoundly moronic moments. "Disraeli wore knickers and practiced swinging a golf club. He whistled frequently, which annoyed Calvin Coolidge, who had affected the dress of a Prussian general from the 1870 war."

These sentences are dreadful enough to demonstrate clearly Hall's courage. He seems willing to try almost anything. He must foresee that a great deal of what he attempts will fail, yet he goes ahead and gives it his best shot. Few contemporary poets of Hall's stature have written so badly; we simply cannot imagine Richard Wilbur or Henry Taylor stepping so clumsily on their cravats as Hall does in the last section of "Eating the Pig," for example, or in "The Wreckage."

But then few other poets are likely to produce an eerie triumph like "The Moon." "A woman who lived / in a tree caught / the moon in a kettle," this poem begins, and it goes on to tell a wonder tale about how the woman boiled the moon down to a bean and ate it, and how it "grew / like a child inside her" until she had to give it birth. Now the woman nurses the moon

> while the wind perches
> like a heavy bird
>
> in the void branches
> of a tree, beside
> a cold kettle.

This haunting little story is presented in diction as simple as Chekhov could muster; the meter is an unobtrusive line of two accents; the syntax is straightforward. The difficulties of conception and composition are apparent only when we consider Hall's purpose—to invent, using entirely traditional folklore, a new legend that accounts for the lunar phases.

It is tempting to dismiss this poet's simpler poems as being too obvious in intention and too easy in execution to bear fruitful close examination. But his simplicity is as deceptive as it is engaging. "Old Timers' Day" is a bit more complex than "The Moon" in its use of simile, but its language and narrative line are just as simple as in the other poem, and its final allusive simile ascends to an effect touching and surprising. The lines report the sight of a favorite baseball player of yesteryear who is taking part in an old timers' game, "laboring forward / like a lame truckhorse" after a fly ball and catching it at the last instant.

> It's a good catch, and the spectators applaud.
> On a green field
> we observe the ruin
> of even the bravest
> body, as Odysseus
> wept to glimpse
> among shades the shadow
> of Achilles.

The animal metaphors that the poem has employed in its earlier lines—truckhorse, filly, gartersnake—have not prepared us for this sudden elevation of comparison, the revelation of heroic dimension. The surprise of the allusion transforms our experience of the poem with a gesture that looks nonchalant, the magician's gesture as he releases a flight of doves from empty air while his audience sits silent with astonishment.

That is my reaction, the feelings of a reader sentimental about baseball and Homer, and there will be others who find the poem a little too calculated, a little too contrived. Yet Hall distrusts contrivance and it is partly because of his ambition to avoid it that he turns to his vatic and surrealist repertoires. He is possessed by natural but contrary urges: to use the poem as a means of exploring new levels of emotion, new planes of discovery, and at the same time to shape it into a dramatic whole. One of his exercises in personification, "The Poem," begins by describing the explorative function: "It discovers by night / what the day hid from it." It ends by affirming the mysteriousness of its subject: "Who knows / what it is thinking?"

Well, the poet knows something of what the poem is thinking. Not because he has written it, but because he has written it many times. And if the poem manages to say something a little different to him each time, the way he hopes it will speak to other less accustomed readers, it also manages to say some of the same things over again. Our ordinary everyday lives are just as mysterious and amazing as the imagination we bring to bear upon them; in fact, there is no ordinary life that is not esoteric at heart.

"The Coffee Cup" takes this latter theme as its subject. Calmly it sets the scene of life in a small New Hampshire town: "The newspaper, the coffee cup, the dog's / impatience for his morning walk: / These fibers braid the ordinary mystery." The lines then record the death and funeral of Anthony "Cat" Middleton, the schoolbus driver, and of his replacement by Mrs. Ek, a woman "with one / eye blue and the other gray." If this New England day were observed from a distance, spatial or historical or sociological, it would be indistinguishable from a thousand other days, its cycle of dying and living repeated as in a corridor of mirrors. But when we see it close up, it displays its mysteriousness in unique details, like the image of Mrs. Ek's eyes. Hall then draws his conclusion, without the skimpiest transition:

> Everything
> is strange; nothing is strange:
> yarn, the moon, gray hair in a bun,
> New Hampshire, putting on socks.

Here is one of those places where the poet must have foreseen that objections would be brought and decided that the risk was necessary. He knew that some persnickety critic would describe the last phrase, "putting on socks," as anticlimactic almost to point of bathos and wayward almost to point of grotesqueness. He knew that another critic would call the phrase preachy and sentimental. But he went ahead and wrote it down and published it.

A composer once confided to me that certain passages of Stravinsky did not bear up well under harmonic analysis. "In fact, some bars look just plain stupid," he said. "All you can do is shrug and say, Well, it's Stravinsky so it must be all right." That's the way I feel about this passage and a number of others: Well, it's Donald Hall so it's probably okay. Lesser poets wouldn't get away with the things he does, but then lesser poets wouldn't attempt them.

Hall's poems allow us to see him in many guises, as Urbane Augustan, Metaphysical Wit, Pastoral Elegist, Biting Satirist, and so on. I don't know that a critic is entitled to prefer one voice over another; it is his duty to give the poet the freedom of the character he chooses to write in. But an admiring reader is permitted to have favorites, and when I place myself in that position I find that I like the Openhearted Christian maybe best of all.

In these days it is nearly impossible to write plain-spoken religious poetry. We have grown addicted to our dim self-doubt and acid ironies, and a simple heartfelt religious lyric is likely to seem falsely ingenuous, unconvincingly childish. We are so unused to the mode that we may think we smell mockery even where we know there is none. Yet such poems can still be written—with a little help perhaps from Anonymous, Ben Jonson, and George Herbert—and, with a little willingness on the part of the reader, they can still be brightly enjoyed. Here is "A Carol":

> The warmth of cows
>   That chewed on hay
> And cherubim
> Protected him
>   As small He lay.
>
> Chickens and sheep
>   Knew He was there
> Because all night
> A holy light
>   Suffused the air.
>
> Darkness was long
>   And the sun brief
> When the Child arose
> A man of sorrows
>   And friend to grief.

Prodigal Son

Louis Simpson stands as an easy example of the poet divided, whose best talents and strongest predilections are at odds with one another. He takes Walt Whitman as spiritual father and his relationship with the figure of Whitman is as troubled and ambiguous as any son's might be with a blood father. He names W. H. Auden as his *bête noire,* although his own best wit and stylishness are closer to Auden's nice effects than to Whitman's woolly dithyrambs.

But perhaps it is not the contrast between the two poets that so exercises him. Simpson struggles with a problem of cultural identity; he has for a long time been trying to define what an American is and then to become one. Whitman represents America, Auden Europe. Louis Simpson's father was British, his mother a Russian Jew, and the lad spent his early years in Jamaica, separated from his parents. In his autobiography, *North of Jamaica,* he identifies America as the place where Mummy was, "a place with tall buildings called skyscrapers" where the inhabitants ate "sugar and bananas."

Already in his miniature verse drama of 1949, "The Arrivistes," a character observes:

> This European scene
> Is like a comedy, each age an act
> In one old plot the public know
> By heart.

From *Chronicles* 13, no. 3 (March 1989). A review of *Collected Poems* by Louis Simpson.

Already in the poem "West" he dreams of "Ranching in Bolinas, that's the life," and in "Mississippi" of rafting down the river with Huck and Jim, "Where old St. Joe slid on the water lights / And on into the dark, diminishing." Already in "Orpheus in America" a sweaty Americanization of European tradition is attempted; "Goodbye to Arcady! / Another world is here, a greener Thrace!"

Yet now when we read the poems of his early period the more European ones seem superior. "The Flight to Cytherea," a homage to Watteau, Baudelaire, and Laforgue, is more successful than "A Farm in Minnesota" or "American Preludes." A straightforward pastiche of Laforgue, "Laertes in Paris," has good moments; the clumsily Yeatsian "The Goodnight" has interesting rhymes, at least; and "The Bird" is as good as most of the ballads by Bertolt Brecht upon which it is modeled. And among these early poems we spot another mentor, too; "Invitation to a Quiet Life" shows more than a hint of W. H. Auden, and "Carentan O Carentan" is imitation pure and naked.

> O Captain, show us quickly
> Our place upon the map.
> But the Captain's sickly,
> And taking a long nap.

Well, what's wrong with that? From whom will a young poet learn if not from the most influential voice of that decade?

Nothing is wrong, nothing at all, if the borrower is gracious enough to acknowledge his debt and to say, as he nowhere does, that once upon a time when he was green and lyric and impressionable the poet W. H. Auden helped to shape the psyche of the organism that calls itself Louis Simpson. He has deigned to praise the youthful Auden for inventing "a compact, elliptical language that was strikingly original" and for being "obscure and prophetic." But he believes that because Auden wrote no confessional poems his work came to lack real substance. "His habitual concealment of his deepest life led him to write in a trivial manner until—at an age when Hardy and Yeats wrote their greatest poems—he was writing light verse."

The review from which I quote these supercilious remarks, "The Split Lives of W. H. Auden," belongs to Simpson's middle period. During this time, the 1970s, Simpson had espoused the notions of poets like Stanley Plumly, Donald Hall, and especially Robert Bly, and believed that poetry had to eschew rhyme and meter and any diction not colloquial. It was to tell dark transcendental secrets of the soul; it was to employ "deep images." He exhibits with ecstatic approval an example from Bly of such stuff: "The lamplight falls on all fours in the grass."

The poem most symptomatic of this middle period is "Walt Whitman at Bear Mountain," in which Simpson carries on a plausible dialogue with a statue of this American bard who has troubled his thoughts for such a long time. "Where are you, Walt?" He complains that the dazzling visions of the future America Whitman promised are abandoned and desecrated. "The Open Road goes to the used-car lot." The mage replies, with a sense of proportion and a humor often lacking in his own poems, that he had not attempted to prophesy or to lay down laws. "I freely confess I am wholly disreputable."

Then the poem breaks down. Some pickpockets and salesmen enter, and then a storekeeper and a housewife are named but not located spatially, and America is unburdened of its "grave weight." This incoherence is concluded with a deep image that Simpson has avowed his pride in: "And the angel in the gate, the flowering plum, / Dances like Italy, imagining red."

The fact that this image makes no sense is, in Simpson's eyes, perhaps the larger part of its glory. He would say of it what he says of Bly's work: "If you are sold on the English department, then this poetry is not for you. You would have a devil of a time trying to explicate it according to the principles of Brooks-and-Warren." But the truth is that it is only in the murkier recesses of English departments that one can find people silly enough to imagine that a poem will be good only so long as Robert Penn Warren cannot understand it.

Beneath his confusions and pretensions there is a streak of thoughtfulness in Simpson, and it is not surprising that he got fed up with the woozy wordgames of this period and desired to write poems about *real* reality, the kind of reality novelists write about, those chaps without fancy language, fancy ideas.

So these days we get poems like "Ed," in which a man drinks too much and wishes he had married a cocktail waitress. Then there is "Bernie," in which a free-spirited fellow writes a successful movie. We get lots of poems with stanzas like this one:

> She is in the middle
> of preparing dinner. Tonight
> she is trying an experiment:
> *Hal Bourgonyaual*—Fish-Potato Casserole.
> She has cooked and drained the potatoes
> and cut the fish in pieces.
> Now she has to "mash potatoes,
> add butter and hot milk," et cetera.

This is camp. It is almost exactly the same kind of camp that Simpson finds the elder Auden guilty of writing. Simpson once announced his intention to write real poems about real people who live in the real world. There are undoubtedly real women who assemble real fish potato casseroles, but they are still waiting for their real poem.

The later poems of Simpson and of Auden boil down to a sort of weakly ironic sociology. In his poem, "The Foggy Lane," Simpson reports upon meeting a "radical" who "wanted to live in a pure world." He also met an insurance agent who claimed that he needed "more protection." The poet elects to join neither of these opposed forces of modern society, but to observe, instead, nature, "the pools made by the rain, / and wheel-ruts, and wet leaves, / and the rustling of small animals." But he only makes of himself a third kind of case history.

In 1955 I met W. H. Auden at a beer joint called Joe's Chili House in Durham, North Carolina. In the course of conversation he flashed, amusedly, an American academic idiom he had obviously acquired only recently. "What," he asked me, "is your major?" "Sociology," I replied, wondering if that mightn't be the case. He made no comment and I felt that I had not struck the right note. I tried a desperate little joke (Brash Freshman

Banters Celebrated Poet). "Or maybe alcoholism," I said. "Well," said he, gazing at me with purblind seriousness, "that's certainly more respectable than sociology."

If, in their later years, Simpson and Auden begin to resemble one another just a little as the infection of sociology makes inroads upon their talents, it may behoove Simpson to show a little more charity toward his fellow *arriviste*. It is only circumstance that Auden is so much the more famous: the best Simpson is almost as good as the best Auden, and his worst is almost as bad as Auden's worst. And like all Americans, native or naturalized, they both have had to work hard to understand what the nation is that they belong to, and what it makes of them.

> In this America, this wilderness
> Where the axe echoes with a lonely sound,
> The generations labor to possess
> And grave by grave we civilize the ground.

Mother Wit

Carolyn Kizer's Humor

It is not often something he has planned, but the overall tone of a lyric poet's collected work is likely to be melancholy. Here are the usual and necessary elegies and the poems of love broken and disappointed; these were sad poems to begin with. But now two decades pass, or three, and over the bitter and furious poems of political protest or personal enmity steals a plangent atmosphere. The anger that roused the poet to heartfelt statement has diminished or transmuted; the former ugly enemy has become a ridiculous or a pathetic figure; and the harsh emotions of the lines now seem overstated, inadequately provoked, and look lost and lonely without their proper causes to back them up. A sadder destiny befalls the poems of friendship. Those bright friends are dead now; the happy poems that celebrated them have turned into dirges.

This common fate has overtaken many of Carolyn Kizer's poems. Her angry poem, "The First of June Again," she must have begun to write in 1966, but the dateline she gives it is no longer angry but tired and resigned: "1966, 1967, 1968, 1969, 1970, and on and on. . . ." "Two Poets by the Lake" is a celebration of a happy occasion and of a shared commitment to the art, but its dedication—"for James Wright"—has affected the genre it belongs to.

It is not that the years have harmed such poems; in fact, the

---

From *An Answering Music*, ed. David Rigsbee (Boston: Ford-Brown and Co., 1990).

changed conditions have added resonance and complexity; these poems—and a good many others of Kizer's—have become richer. But they have lost their innocence; they are no longer the same pure outcries of bitterness or of warm delight as when they were first set down. And though the poems may have become better for the changes that have taken place in the world, yet there is something sad in the simple fact of those changes.

The humorous poem withstands this specific kind of change. It may become stale if its humor was not bright enough in the first place, or it may become pointless when its cause or occasion is forgotten. Sometimes it comes to seem callow or heartless, as many of Thomas Hood's poems have done, when modes of humor change. But it rarely becomes sad unless sadness was originally a part of its humor, as in the case of some of Blake's poems.

Carolyn Kizer's humorous poems have resisted the change to sadness, though they have changed in other ways. Many of the poems of witty and trenchant observation have become rather doctrinal as trends of attitude have caught up with them. The 1984 volume, *Mermaids in the Basement,* is avowedly feminist ("I thank dear friends everywhere, feminists all," the poet's endnote says), but most of the poems it contains have been around for quite a long while, successful without the easy label.

The label is still inadequate. The first three parts of the famous "Pro Femina" can as easily be read as anti-feminist as pro. This answer to Juvenal's Satire against Women owes a little too much to the acid Roman to be heavily pro anything. But Kizer has added a fourth part, "Fanny," a long courageous interior monologue attributed to Robert Louis Stevenson's wife, as if to show the other side of the coin, to show what the situation is really like—and this addition has changed the thrust of the poem.

Not entirely for the better perhaps. For though "Fanny" has added richness and pathos to the work, it has also blunted some of the sharp observation and acute formulation that give "Pro Femina" its zest. Of the poets of our time Kizer is the only one to capture much of the spirit of Juvenal, his plain language and broadsword wit and pinpoint characterization. Set "Pro Femina" beside Robert Lowell's adaption of Juvenal's Tenth Satire and see how pale Kizer makes it look.

For on one side of her talent Kizer is a true Roman. In "A Muse" and "Plaint of the Poet in an Ignorant Age," she laments her lack of classical learning, but probably she exaggerates. There is a certain English traditional tone of Juvenal and Horace which Kizer approaches and, oddly, it is in her adaptations from the Chinese that she is most nearly Horatian, in such poems as "Hiding Our Love," "Amusing Our Daughters," and "For Jan, in Bar Maria."

But the Juvenalian manner is more deliberately apparent than the Horatian:

> I will speak of women of letters, for I'm in the racket.
> Our biggest successes to date? Old maids to a woman.
> And our saddest conspicuous failures? The married spinsters
> On loan to the husbands they treated like surrogate fathers.
> Think of that crew of self-pitiers, not-very-distant,
> Who carried the torch for themselves and got first-degree
> burns.
> Or the sad sonneteers, toast-and-teasdales we loved at
> thirteen;
> Middle-aged virgins seducing the puerile anthologists
> Through lust-of-the-mind; barbituate-drenched Camilles
> With continuous periods, murmuring softly on sofas
> When poetry wasn't a craft but a sickly effluvium,
> The air thick with incense, musk, and emotional blackmail.

Her heavily anapestic five-stress lines with their central caesurae imitate the noise of Latin hexameters very convincingly, and this technical feat alone persuades me that she knows Latin verse. But it is in the swift and accurate characterizations that the poem shines most brightly, the compound epithets fixing the personalities once and for all: "toast-and-teasdales," "middle-aged virgins," "barbiturate-drenched Camilles." She has the classic, or neoclassic, ability to make a broad generalization compact and immediate—and deadly. The first line announces the subject, adding a note of easy self-deprecation. The condition of the female literary life is then exhibited by no fewer than five sharply distinguished examples, and the stanza ends by gathering itself into a characterization of a whole literary era and attitude. There is indignation, even a faint disgust, in her motives, but the deftness and polish of the lines keep these feelings at an elegant distance.

And all along the way are rapier touches: paradoxes (Our biggest successes?—Old maids), oxymorons ("married spinsters"), and puns ("toast-and teasdales," "continuous periods"). She makes one nice joke by transforming figurative language into literal event—"Who carried the torch for themselves and got first-degree burns"—and another by parodying the cozy alliterative mumble of the Georgians, "murmuring softly on sofas." The last line is a nifty example of that classical trope called "zeugma": *incense, musk,* and *blackmail.*

Best of all, she has the self-confidence of the satirist. She can make statements, sweeping generalizations, fearlessly, and then give the straightforward impulse of her thought unexpected twists, as in "married spinsters / *On loan.*" She knows too how to place the Billingsgate adjective where it will do the most damage: "surrogate fathers," "sad sonneteers," "sickly effluvium."

What everyone has always said is probably true, that there is nothing so leaden as analysis of humor. But I am not so much interested here in analysis as I am in simply expressing the grounds for my admiration, because I have the impression that appreciation for this particular kind of humor is not prevalent in this dour decade. The mass audience taste for humor seems to run toward the sophomoric hysterics of "Saturday Night Live," while our poets seem content with limp anecdotes and pallid little ironies. The free and open mockery of neoclassic satire is not merely unfashionable, but may be almost incomprehensible nowadays. The university literature courses in Swift and Pope go begging for students. Kizer's talent for Augustan humor is the more refreshing as it has become a rarity.

One of her funniest poems, "Running Away from Home," is positively Hogarthian with its gallery of character types. Here she is intent on portraying every sort of genuine loser to be found in the American northwest, the ones driven crazy by idleness and religion as well as the ones who are lunatic by accident or choice. She is especially sharp in depicting the terror and hypocrisy of the teenaged girls:

> *Dear Sally, Dear Beth, Dear Patsy, Dear Eileen,*
> Pale, faceless girls, my best friends at thirteen,
> Knelt on cold stone, with chilblained knees, to pray,
> "Dear God, Dear Christ! Don't let him go All the Way!"

And, as she often does, Kizer encapsulates the larger situation in a specific character type:

> We still carry those Rosary scars, more like a *herpes*
> *Simplex* than a stigmata: give us a nice long fit
> Of depression; give us a good bout of self-hate;
> Give us enough Pope, we pun, and we'll hang.
>
> Hung, well hung, or hungover, in the world's most durable
> Morning after, we'd sooner keep the mote and lose the eye.
> Move over, Tonio Kröger, you never attended
> Our Lady of Sorrows, or Northwestern High!

The reminiscence of Louis MacNeice in that last couplet points forward to the fourth section, the Montana section, of the poem where mocking allusions form part of the humor. Stephen Spender, Dylan Thomas, Shelley, and G. M. Hopkins are playfully mutilated: "I think continually of those who are truly crazy"; "But they're still Missoula / In their craft and sullen ebbing"; "Taint the white radiance of O'Leary's brain"; "Couple-colored as her old brindled cat."

In "A Muse" the poet admits that she has been, "almost from birth, irresistibly drawn to the bad pun." That fact, on the evidence of her verse, is undeniable. Along with "enough Pope," "Running Away" includes such other horrors as "the flammable Museum / Of Modern Mart" and "running off at the scars"—though the latter is so farfetched I'm not sure it can be called a pun.

"To a Visiting Poet in a College Dormitory" includes two punning allusions: "having gathered all / Your strength into one battered bowling ball" and "Loves are interred three deep, or rise like drowned / Ruined choristers." In "Semele Recycled" there is a truly horrid one, "all eyes." In "The Apostate" we find that "careful Harry [Heinrich Heine] / Stood by the flames with his bucket of sand, / Passing out pogroms—er—programs for his Farewell Tour."

And there are other puns as bad, or worse, scattered throughout her work, but this sample is probably more than sufficient for delicate readers. (I must emphasize, though, that Kizer's bad puns purposely contribute to the self-deprecatory tone of the poems. She is not *merely* sadistic.)

Her ironies, then, are broad and often savage. But this is not always the case. She is able to mute her gifts to a gentler and slyer mode, the more prevailing mode in contemporary poetry, which owes perhaps the greater part of its authority to John Crowe Ransom. "The Patient Lovers" is tinged with Ransom's influence, and so too, I think, is the title poem of Kizer's first volume, *The Ungrateful Garden.*

In this poem the curse of the gift he asked for has already fallen upon mythological King Midas; everything he touches turns to gold. For this reason he hates the out-of-doors, where his lawns are "a wilderness of noise, / The heavy clang of leaf on leaf." The artificial indoors is comfy and reassuring, but natural objects, transforming to metal, treat him cruelly. Golden stubble cuts his feet.

> Dazzled with wounds, he limped away
> To climb into his golden bed.
> Roses, roses can betray.
> "Nature is evil," Midas said.

"The Ungrateful Garden" may well be a perfect poem of its kind. Kizer has delivered the myth with stringent economy and—importantly—in its own terms. But she has emphasized certain elements of it so that new interpretations are possible. The myth that formerly seemed only a moralizing fable about greed has been transformed into a broadly applicable, paradigmatic allegory about—well, let us say it is about the human incapacity to engage with nature in nature's own terms. Having transformed nature into the stuff of his own shortsighted desires, Midas now finds it cruel and alien; "the rude / Gold thorn has made his fingers bleed." The narrative remains an attack on materialism, but when we think of modern developments in technology and the philosophy of science, we see that Kizer has given it a slant both wide-ranging and highly specific. She has kept the fable timeless while simultaneously making it pointedly contemporary.

Kizer has written other poems which reinterpret mythological material—"Semele Recycled," for example, and "Hera, Hung from the Sky" and "Persephone Pauses"—but generally in these examples her method is one of straightforward comment, though her humor is never entirely absent.

It is doubtful, in fact, that humor is entirely absent from any of her work, even the most serious. "The Blessing" is an attempt to come to terms with the ravaging experience of having been a daughter to a passionate mother while now being a passionate mother to a grieving daughter. It is an intense and searching and often sorrowful poem, a poem which pulls no punches. Yet even its darkest lines are lightened with grotesquely humorous detail.

> My mother's dust has rested
> for fifteen years
> in the front hall closet
> because we couldn't bear to bury it.
> Her dust-lined, dust-coated urn
> squats among the size-eleven overshoes.

Kizer seems to look upon humor as one of the most welcome parts of her personal, as well as her human, heritage. It is for her not only necessary for balance and tolerance, it a necessity for survival. When she thinks of the gifts her mother bestowed upon her, humor is one of them for which she feels most grateful, and one she would wish to pass on to others.

> Child and old woman
> soothing each other,
> sharing the same face
> in a span of seventy years,
> the same mother wit.

My remarks here are hardly exhaustive. I have not spoken of the poet's use of the extended witty conceit in poems like "Food of Love," and other poems like "Bitch" and "Children" also deserve comment in regard to humor. But I am pleased to point toward one of Carolyn Kizer's most generous qualities and to bless my good luck in enjoying it in her work, a luck I can almost equate with "the luck of our husbands and lovers, who keep free women."

"Out of the Hills of Certainty"

Miller Williams's Skeptical Science

Miller Williams has produced some of the genuinely humorous poems of our time, along with some of the most passionate love lyrics, in colloquial language of fine nuance and hard power. But when his poems turn to large philosophical concerns they are likely to employ the hypotheses and conclusions of contemporary science, as well as its terminology, in order to reveal the poet's pervasive and enduring skepticism.

The paradox inherent in this method, this usage of the language of precision and certainty in order to exhibit and explore Williams's distrust of impersonal data and of all generalization, is entirely in keeping with his insistent playfulness, his thorough questioning of the value and purpose of intellectual striving. Williams's attitude toward intellectual endeavor is largely ambiguous, but perhaps it could be formulated in crude terms in the following sentence: Man can never know truth but he is damned if he doesn't try to. And damned also if he does try.

A more graceful presentation of some aspects of this skepticism is the epigrammatic poem "It's Hard to Think the Brain":

> It's hard to think the brain
> a ball of ropey dough
> should have invented pain
> or come to know

---

how there are things we lend
a fragile credence to
and hope to comprehend
but never do.

Williams repeatedly advances the notion that the objective truths we think we have discovered by dint of determined effort are only constructions of the mind, ideations that may amount to no more than subjective fantasies. In "Some Lines Finished Just Before Dawn at the Bedside of a Dying Student It Has Snowed All Night" he throws doubt on the prevalent concept of a four-dimensional space-time continuum:

Some Physicists believe in four
planes of space. This is more
than we can know, lacking the sense
to see the plane our reason bends
about the other three. This
is not called faith. That's what it is.

It is called, of course, not faith but science. But since this scientific construct depends entirely upon something, a fourth dimension, that the senses cannot apprehend, it is an object of faith. God, too, is an object of faith, the poem goes on to say, so why shouldn't we believe in God? Come to that, why shouldn't we believe in any object of faith?

And cherubim and seraphim?
Ghosts and ogres? Vampires? Elves?
People who can turn themselves
to cats and make potatoes rot
and curdle a mother's milk? Why not?

In this poem Williams rages at the limits of knowledge because they limit the range of the speaker's sympathies. He cannot enter into the dying student's experience; he cannot imagine what the experience must be like, and compares the failure of his imagination to a dimming light in which subjective phantasms are glimpsed.

Already the light when I turn that way
is dim. Sometimes I see the shapes
of people flying. Or clouds, perhaps.
Or trees. Or houses. Or nothing at all.

The feeling of drained helplessness that the speaker articulates in this poem is found in many of the poems that deal with the problem of knowledge. In "The Associate Professor Delivers an Exhortation to His Failing Students" the speaker is possessed by such a thorough skepticism in regard to the possibility of knowledge that he comes near to despair. He warns his students about "getting hung up in the brain's things / that send you screaming like madmen through the town." He claims that any girl "anonymous as beer" encountered in a bar could have taught his subject as well as he. He avers that "there is no Jesus and no hell," that "all the answers at best are less than half." He advises his audience that their surest hope is to abandon hope.

The day I lectured on adrenalin
I meant to tell you
as you were coming down
slowly out of the hills of certainty
empty your mind of the hopes that held you there.

Miller Williams seems at first glance willing, and even anxious, to push an unnerving skepticism to the limit. He shows little faith in scientific method. The laboratory frogs the associate professor refers to in his exhortation are regarded as having given their lives "for nothing" and "are washed from the brains and pans / we laid them in." In his most ambitious essay at the problem, the long poem called "Notes from the Agent on Earth: How to Be Human," he refers to the scientist as "the pither of frogs and cat-slitter." And the characterizations of scientists throughout his poems show them as confused, depressed, despairing, or even, in one teasing love poem ("The Assoc. Professor [Mad Scientist] to [His Love] His Student in Physics 100 Lab"), as crazy.

It is not only scientific knowledge that Williams lacks faith in. Philosophy and art are equally untrustworthy. In "The Proper Study" the practice of introspection as the method of the mystic, the psychologist, and the philosopher is seen as presenting us only with phantasmagoric and meaningless images in place of truth, "a blue anteater with seven heads," for example, and an "aged mother / rocking in her lap a pig." But when the seeker turns his attention outward, when he investigates the objects of nature as an astronomer, he finds after staring at a star with his "biggest telescope" that "it's not a star, it's not a star, it's a hole!" Both methods of investigation yield up either illusion or disillusion.

In the poem "He Speaks to His Arguing Friends and to Himself" the discussion shifts to ontology. "There is no question / except the question of final cause." The poet considers two possibilities, the first being that the universe came into being ex nihilo, from "pure unplace." He cannot bring himself to believe this notion. "This is one impossible road." The other impossible road is to believe in God. "Imagine a mind that always was, / where *In the beginning* makes no sense. / Think it thinks us into being." The speaker finds neither alternative convincing. "Either way you'd bet not."

Even so, even though he is faced with two impossibilities of which neither offers advantage over the other, the speaker chooses between them; he chooses to believe in God. His choice seems at first glance a resigned one caused by what William James referred to as "failure of nerve."

> But we have believed through such pain
> and made such music for so long
> that it would be a hurt and shame
> if we should learn that we were wrong.
> We have enough to fret about.
> Almost all of us concur,
> we'll live with the holidays we have
> and the grace of God as if it were.

Yet the choice here is not resigned or arbitrary or cynical; it proceeds from a different but closely related current of Williams's thought, a strand of his thought that is concerned with the nature of systems and with the possibility of affirmation.

The first alternative offered us in "He Speaks to His Arguing Friends" is not the old-fashioned one of creation happening merely by means of utter chance. Williams refers instead to the very recent idea that nothingness is in itself a creative force, that it is actually in the nature of the void to give rise to physical being. He describes this "pure unplace" in witty terms, then says, "Imagine that it all explodes / (although there's nothing to explode) / till matter and energy come to be."

Williams's grounding in science, whether it is a professional technical grounding or not, looks to be pretty thorough and up-to-date. New theories amuse him and sometimes bemuse him, and he handles them with ease and often with relaxed humor. Perhaps he is able to do so because he puts so little faith in them as final answers; in fact, he would seem to wish to reject final answers even if they could be found. Perhaps he imagines for mankind the happy destiny of never making a conclusive choice among metaphysical possibilities. In one poem he congratulates the euglena, that unicellular flagellate that biologists classify sometimes as a plant and sometimes as an animal, for evading the definite choice of phylum and surviving because of that evasion:

> Fencerider,
>
> you've held your own for twenty
> million years
> who might have been a tulip
> or a tiger
>
> you shrewd little bastard.

If neither philosophical introspection nor scientific investigation can provide absolutely certain data, if final metaphysical choices ought to be evaded or selected for the sake of human convenience and spiritual comfort, then not much is left objectively to believe in, except for that one organ or faculty or talent which enables us to believe—that is, the mind itself. There is a constructivist flavor to Williams's thought; he may owe more than has been remarked to Alfred North Whitehead. We make up our minds about reality and, having done so, have made up reality.

Williams likes not only to compare but to equate the so-called objective nature of science and the subjective nature of poetry. In an early poem, "Level IV," he takes the physicists' definition of "work" as a definition of poetry: "there is a change / in temperature." The associate professor in his fervid exhortation makes the same kind of comparison between science and poetry.

> The day you took the test
> I would have told you this:
> that you had no time to listen for questions
> hunting out the answers in your files
> is surely the kind of irony
> poems are made of

Not only is one intellectual system as valid as any other in this benevolent skeptical view, they are all equal in purpose, method, and result; they are interchangeable in terms of a grand algorithmic superstructure. The terms of metaphor—that is, of analogy—are not only interchangeable, in Williams's view, they are interdependent. In his poem "Form and Theory of Poetry" the pattern of traffic around a football stadium at game time is used to describe the thermodynamic career of a hurricane. Then the analogy of the hurricane is used to describe the complex motions associated with a football game and its spectators. "Form and Theory" is a curious, centerless poem that arouses in a reader an odd relativistic sensation because neither term of the metaphor is stable. An ordinary poetic metaphor will compare this girl here and now to that rose there and then; one term is taken as literal, the other as imaginary. In Williams's poem both terms, football game and hurricane, describe one another interchangeably; both terms are simultaneous and timeless at once; both terms are literal and imaginary at once.

Think in the eye of a hurricane, then, of Tittle,
Thorpe and Namath, Simpson, such acts of God.
At a football game, think of the gulf coast,
Biloxi, Mississippi blown away.

This relativism of analogical terms enables widely disparate systems of thought to illuminate, illustrate, and validate one another because it makes them all equal as metaphoric terms in poetic structures.

This idea is dealt with more explicitly in "Believing in Symbols," which advances the proposition that all intellectual ideas are derived from a single idea. Williams's image for this notion is the number 8 as we find it in the display of a digital calculator. The speaker of the poem has put a calculator into the pocket of his shirt, over his heart, where it has shorted out. "That afternoon / it lay on my desk and turned out 8s for hours." He considers them as two symbols, the calculator representing science, the heart representing emotional life or the life of the spirit: "So what do we say for science and the heart? / So with reason the heart will have its way?" He then makes a humorous point about this Pascalian dichotomy and passes on to ponder, in the second half of the poem, the nature of symbols.

All the numbers, "1 through 7, also nothing and 9," can be formed by lighting up portions of the two stacked squares that compose the digital 8. This 8 is "the figure all the figures are made from"; it is "the enabling number, the all-fathering," although (and also because) it "is only itself." He finds other likenesses for the number—the self-enclosing single-surfaced Möbius strip, and the sidewise 8, ∞, which is the mathematical symbol for infinity—and in these guises too the 8 is "all-fathering."

The succession of digital numbers inside the framework of the 8 reminds the speaker of successive eras of history, which also take place inside an inescapable frame. "The pterodactyl, Pompeii, the Packard; / things take their turns." Numbers that once held mystic and religious meanings are seen to be only emphasized parts of the one superstructural figure; "3 and 7 are only / numbers again." Looking back to his calculator/

heart symbolism, he characterizes historic eras as being dominated either by reason or by emotion—and then declares that the opposition between the rational and the irrational is specious, and may even be illusionary.

> Not to say that physics will ever fail us
> or plain love, either, for that matter.
> Like the sides of a coin, they may take turns,
> or flipping fast enough, may seem to merge.

The poem next pursues the image of the flipped coin spinning in the air. The dichotomies melt together; heads or tails, reason or unreason, it all amounts to the same thing. It is a game of chance. However you think about reality, your terms are equally correct and incorrect, equally viable and equally useless. Whatever terms you may invent are inadequate and inapplicable. When you gamble by flipping a coin you lose because you call heads but tails comes up. In Williams's game you lose because heads-or-tails doesn't matter; heads is wrong, and tails is wrong too.

> Call it, if you call it, in the air.
> When the coin comes down, the tent comes down.
> You look around, and there is nothing there.
> Not even the planets. Not even the names of the planets.

Every shred of certainty is stripped away—the science that discovers the planets, the history and mythology that are employed to name them. The traveling carny game is over; the tent comes down.

The poet's conclusion is a bleak one for those who have put their faith in the spurious declarations of philosophy and science. Any truth that was ever gained is interchangeable with any other truth; all is relative. In "Notes from the Agent on Earth: How to Be Human" Williams finds another image (it is a variation upon Lucretius's illustrative argument for an infinite unverse) for the relativistic point of view. The undefined place where each of us stands seems to someone else a well-defined horizon.

> What matters most in survival is learning the names
> of things and the names of visions. If the horizon
> for an example were real someone could go there
> and call back to the rest of us and say
> Here we are standing on the horizon.
> But he would see that his friends were standing on it.

Yet the vision is not entirely cheerless. This stanza about the relative horizon begins with an affirmative statement: "There is much that matters. What matters most is survival." And, after considering the relativistic paradoxes of space-time, the poem examines our attempts to avoid the bitterness of the paradoxes by means of self-induced illusion and then adjures us to eschew illusion so that we may attain the primary value of survival. The memories we keep of time past "are illusions, or seem to be illusions. / Leave them alone. What matters most is survival."

Miller Williams belongs to that class of poets who feel compelled to tell us things they know we are not eager to hear. Lucretius is a poet of this sort, and so are George Crabbe, Thomas Hardy, and Robinson Jeffers. Yet, if we could be persuaded to give up our illusions, they seem to say, there might be some point in our vain hopes, in all our earnest fruitless striving.

The poem "Entropy" may be understood to set forth this position. The first four sentences describe in thoughtful and humorous metaphors and images the relentless consequences of the Second Law of Thermodynamics; but the final two words of the poem may allow our efforts and hopes a glimmer of legitimacy and efficacy. "Intend," says Williams twice, echoing in striking fashion the final injunction of Robert Frost's "Provide, Provide," and echoing too Frost's grim tone. The imperative here exhorts the friends to give their greetings with all purposeful good will, with genuinely amicable feeling. Even if nothing is accomplished, even if everything must expire at last, it makes a difference for us to mean well toward one another and toward existence as a whole. The blind scientific facts that make up the universe will not be changed by even our best intentions. But our best intentions are admirable and make a difference in the complexion that can be put upon things. So Miller Williams implies in this poem, and if this thought is not the happiest a poet has ever brought to us, it is as sanguine as this unflinchingly tough-minded poet can make it.

Entropy

You say Hello and part of what you spend
to say it goes to God. There is a tax
on all our simplest thoughts and common acts.
It will come to pass that friend greets friend
and there is not a sound. Thus God subtracts
bit by little bit till in the end
there is nothing at all. Intend. Intend.

Paz

Upon a confirmed gringo like me, contemporary Spanish language poetry makes much the same impression as contemporary Spanish or Latin American concert music. Broad prairies of cadenza enclose a garden patch of melodic theme, an orotund thunder of flourish results in a brief shower of substance. The treacherous mellifluousness of Spanish cloaks even the most shocking and brutal of utterance with a lyric sangfroid. For some intangible reason, it becomes hard to take Spanish language literature as seriously as other modern literatures. There is no solid reason that the works of Heinrich Böll and William Golding should be better known than those of Pio Baroja—but they are.

This supranational critical neglect has endured for a long time now, but there is a possibility that in our time three writers may have restored some measure of justice to the appreciation of Latin American literature. These writers are Jorge Luis Borges, Gabriel Garcia Márquez, and Octavio Paz.

This trio of names will irritate Paz. He does not count Brazilian writers or the Portuguese language as belonging to the Latin American tradition. He is fed to the teeth—like most of his colleagues—with the name of Borges, but perhaps he does not recognize that for many of us much of the importance of Borges lies in the fact that he was denied the Nobel Prize because of his conservative political views. That injustice

---

From *Chronicles* 13, no. 3 (March 1989). Review of *The Collected Poems of Octavio Paz, 1957–1987,* edited by Eliot Weinberger, and of *Convergences: Essays on Art and Literature* by Octavio Paz.

still rankles even in my own bleeding-heart liberal breast. And I think that Paz would not like to find himself designated as standard bearer for Latin American literature if there were any hint of programmatic insularity or provincialism connected with that honor.

Octavio Paz is quite consciously a global poet, one whose reputation is unhobbled by national boundaries. We have had precious few poets with such magnitude of repute since the time of Pound, Eliot, and Auden. Stephen Spender is still with us, and in the United States we have Robert Penn Warren; Russia boasts of Yevtushenko, but his work is not much respected by other poets. And these are about all the world class bards we have on hand, aren't they?

Perhaps not—but in whatever list we set down, Octavio Paz will be included, and he will stand out among the other names as one who deliberately fashioned himself into this kind of poet, a man who realized there was a choice to be made, a position to fill.

There was first of all the matter of apprenticeship. We cannot say that Paz is the disciple of any single poet in the way that we can describe Robert Hillyer and William Meredith as disciples of Robert Frost. Paz took the whole modernist hagiology as his example and has tried to make personal acquaintance with as many of these figures as possible. In dedications to poems and in incidental remarks in critical essays, we find the names of Pierre Reverdy, Luis Cernuda, André Breton, John Cage, Roger Caillois, Robert Motherwell, Vasko Popa, Albert Camus, and many, many others—even Robert Frost, who seems almost bumptiously out of place in this aggregate of intellectual fashion plates. Paz studied the works of these artists, found opportunity to meet them, questioned them, and took from them all that he profitably could.

In a North American poet this procedure might well appear sycophantic, but to Paz it was necessary. He found Mexico a culturally backward country, he regarded himself in his earliest years as something of an outsider, and he saw the modernist tradition as a set of doctrines for which he could serve as evangelist. He need not—indeed, he did not—espouse all the ideas he imported and explained, but he was attracted to a great many of them and has enjoyed cheerful flirtation with scores of concepts which contradict one another. Paz is a Don Juan of the intellect. His thought is articulate, passionate, and extremely eclectic, but it is not profound; he takes such sensual enjoyment of so many ideas that he cannot bear to form a lasting relationship with any of them.

Romanticism, socialism, Freudianism, surrealism, Buddhism, Hinduism, cubism, Jungian archetypes, regionalism, dada, expressionism, haiku, renga, ballad, folk song, pun, rhyme, free verse, Donne, Gongora, Whitman, Sade, Quevedo, even Samuel Johnson (whom he wildly misunderstands)—all these impulses, tendencies, isms, itches, notions, whims, motives, concepts, tics, and frotheries have received at least passing attention from Paz. He has proclaimed and explained and declaimed and disowned and denied and decried all of these and many more besides. If sixteenth-century Euphuism showed its flowery countenance upon the earth once again, Paz would probably have a weekend fling with it.

Such ideological philandering marks Paz as lacking the highest philosophical seriousness, but at the same time it helps to make him a powerful and valuable artist. He is a better surrealist poet for not submitting to doctrinaire surrealist policy as pronounced by André Breton or Max Ernst or anyone else. When he is a nationalist poet, he is more deeply regional for placing his work directly in the tradition of the European avant-garde. When he is a concrete poet, making poems in which the most apparent interest is visual design, he gives these productions point by rooting them in the peculiarities of the Spanish language. While it is true that he has deliberately searched out the most fashionable of intellectual fads of our time, he has been able to turn all of them to personal expression and to nobler purpose than they ordinarily enjoy. *Materiem superabat opus,* yes; but in Paz what the artistry transcends is not the materials but the mannerisms that usually accompany a certain style.

In a poet so many-minded it is impossible to find lines that might accurately be designated as "typical," but perhaps this stanza from "One Day Among Many" can give a characteristic impression of Paz's surrealism:

> The cars are nostalgic for grass
> Towers walk
>   time has stopped
> A pair of eyes won't leave me alone
> they are an agate beach in the calcined south
> they are the sea between the rocks the color of rage
> they are the fury of June and its shawl of bees

There is nothing finally distinctive about these phrases, which could as easily have been written by Breton or Paul Eluard or René Char; this is the common idiom of surrealists, interchangeable among poets as well as among poems.

But Paz has seen through this style so thoroughly that he has produced, in "This and This and This," a telling parody. The poem begins, as surrealist poems so often do, with a portentously self-gratulatory overstatement, "Surrealism has been the apple of fire on the tree of syntax." A long litany of absurd and bombastic claims follows—"Surrealism has been the cardboard crown on the headless critic and the viper that slips between the legs of the critic's wife"—and climaxes in a hysterical overview of modern history: "Surrealism has been the seven-league boots of those who escaped from the prisons of dialectical reason and Tom Thumb's hatchet that severs the knots of the poisonous vines that cover the walls of the petrified revolutions of the Twentieth Century." When surrealist poetry begins to sound like a Woody Allen character trying to write a surrealist poem, we know the jig is up.

Not that the possibilities of surrealist style are exhausted for Paz, not at all. His work is always going to be marked in some degree by fantastic hyperbole. But surrealism is to be counted as merely one more style, one more useful weapon in the poet's varied arsenal; for Paz it is neither a religion or a politics, as it was for those figures of the 1930s who now look so dated. I am thinking of the early Luis Buñuel, the early

Marcel Duchamp, the early Louis Aragon; I am thinking of *Un Chien Anadalou.*

But Paz can remember the rovlutionaries of that period, political and artistic, in darker terms. He speaks of them in a poem of the 1970s, "San Idlefonso nocturne":

> Good, we wanted good:
>   to set the world right.
> We didn't lack integrity:
>   we lacked humility.
> What we wanted was not innocently wanted.
> Precepts and concepts,
>   the arrogance of the theologians,
> to beat with a cross,
>   to institute with blood,
> to build the house with bricks of blood,
> to declare obligatory communion.
>   Some
> became secretaries to the secretary
> to the General Secretary of the Inferno.
>   Rage
> became philosophy,
>   its drivel has covered the planet.

The warmest attraction of these lines is the evident fact that they are written more in sorrow than in anger. The belated recognition of common human frailty in the youthful utopists is a fresh theme and genuinely pathetic. In order to write these lines, the poet has had first to experience, and then to overcome, his weary disillusionment. He may abhor the outcome of reckless idealism (in this line from "Although It Is Night" he refers to Stalin's purges: "Utopia comes to earth in the Camps"), but he does not despise the idealists.

In fact, in his remarks about the weakling state of contemporary poetry in the world, he is both shrewd and sympathetic. In "The Verbal Contract," a public address published in *Convergences,* he says, "I imagine that the timidity of today's poets is due, among other things, to sheer fatigue: for more than half a century we have devoted all our energies to frenetic formal experimentation in the arts. It is a commonplace that these successive movements have degenerated into sterile manipulation: the avant-garde today repeats itself endlessly and has become a form of academicism."

One of the peculiarities of Paz's proposed regimen—as it is of his career—is that an artist is to begin as a member of the avant-garde and then to graduate from that brilliant but shallow cosmopolitanism into work that is more individual, more personal, more local. I am reminded of the story about Duke Ellington and the experimental jazz bass player Charles Mingus, when they were preparing to produce a recording together. "Hey, man," Mingus said, "let's do some avant-garde music." "Aw no," Ellington replied, "let's do something *modern.*" All those literary and artistic isms that Paz has been involved with appear to have been procedures he made himself learn in order to be able to forget. He begins to look through the predictable future into the unpredictable past.

"We are returning to diversity," he declares. "This is one of the few positive signs in this terrible end of a century. Uniformity is death, and the most perfect form of uniformity is universal death; hence the collective extermination practiced in the twentieth century. Life is always particular and local: it is *my* life, this life of mine here and now. The resurrection of national and regional cultures is a sign of life."

Reflecting upon these words, we are not surprised to recall that one of Paz's almost constant heroes is Charles Fourier. The specifics of Fourier's utopia he rejects as unworkable and in the end as undesirable. But the ambition to humanize technology, to make it responsive to individual needs and desires, remains supremely valuable in his eyes. It becomes clear that for Paz avant-garde artistic movements are like technologies which the artist must master and subdue and bend to his own purposes. His cheerily restless experimentation has amounted to a lifetime of apprenticeship needed to fashion a skill, or even a genius, which could define and express the soul and body of his native Mexico, the collective spirit of Latin America.

The work that embodies these great aims will never be written. Paz fits into that modern romantic tradition in which the poet's great work remains unfinished. Romanticism is a mode of discourse which gives us hope by breaking its promises, and many of its greatest figures trace incomplete careers. Coleridge, Keats, Rimbaud, Hölderlin, Lorca—the pantheon of maimed titans is a large one. Like his great precursors, Paz understands that the only way to get the highest expression out of art is to demand more of it than it has to give. To this end, he keeps on defining and redefining poetry in his work. There must be scores of separate, and differing, definitions of the poetic art in his essays and poems. This one, from "San Idlefonso nocturne," may serve to help define Octavio Paz for us and to illustrate the noble shapes his thought and feeling can take:

> Poetry,
> suspension bridge between history and truth,
> is not a path toward this or that:
> it is to see
> the stillness in motion,
> change
> in stillness.
> History is the path:
> it goes nowhere,
> we all walk it,
> truth is to walk it.
> We neither go nor come:
> we are in the hands of time.
> Truth:
> to know ourselves,
> from the beginning,
> hung.
> Brotherhood over the void.

On Process: An Interview

You once described your writing process as beginning with a look at notes you'd scribbled on paper, ideas you'd jotted down. When you write down these ideas, or when you pick them up again, do you know at the outset whether they'll turn into poem or story?

Not always. I have a notion that something is going to be either a poem or a story before I begin writing it, but during the process of writing sometimes this notion changes. A number of stories have turned into poems and vice versa. When I used material I'd planned to put in a long poem called *Midquest,* I found that some of this turned to short stories, and later on evolved into a novel called *I Am One of You Forever.* So it's not entirely possible to say, but generally I know what I want to write. Whether I'm actually able to write it or not is impossible to predict.

You encourage your students to experiment with both poetry and fiction, perhaps to rewrite a poem as a short story or vice versa. How often do you do this yourself?

Not too often, although sometimes I will include the material of a poem in a short story. I find that change of form changes the material entirely so that sometimes it's unrecognizable as the same material. The form makes so much difference, and

---

This interview was conducted by Melissa Brannon on July 9, 1992, in Greensboro, North Carolina. Brannon is poetry editor of *The Greensboro Review* and has published poems in various literary magazines.

the feelings we bring to the form, not only as writers, but as readers too, that what seems to be kind of the same experience turns out not to be the same. Writers are liable to use the same material in poems and stories without realizing it. It's very instructive to read through Poe on this account, because he often did use the same material. And so did a number of the French writers of the late ninteenth century; the material was plastic; they could use it in any form. Most people, however, limit themselves to writing in one form, and so they don't think about other possibilities. It's more likely, to tell the truth, that the material for a poem would go into a novel rather than a short story because there's a way in which you need a large mosaic of the kind of experiences you have in poems in order to give a novel emotional depth. And a short story has its own emotional fabric, so that if there is any dislocation or any undue emphasis on single events in short stories, it's liable to overbalance a short story, ruin the texture of it.

Why do you think many writers limit themselves to either poetry or fiction?

I think they have vocations; I think you're called to write fiction or you're called to write poetry or you're called to write drama or you're called to write nonfiction, and it's only an odd few people who began writing very early in their lives and trained themselves in more than one form. I frankly would not recommend to a younger writer to write in both forms. I would say go one way or the other.

Try them both when you're young, but settle on one or the other?

Yes, experiment just to see what the feeling is. The reason to use both forms when you're young is the same reason to learn a foreign language. You learn to think with a different area of your senses, your experience, some different side of your sensibility. And you never know what's there until you poke around a little bit. But when you've decided what you're called to write, then that's the thing to stick with, I think. I'm speaking in purely professional terms, of course. I have to admit, though, that many famous writers, fiction writers, write secret poetry and don't show it to anybody. A lot of writers do that. I'll mention Peter Taylor right off the bat, but there are lots more too.

When you're writing fiction, do you take breaks from it to write a poem, or do you concentrate on one form at a time?

I try to concentrate on one at a time. Sometimes you have requests; somebody wants a poem for a special occasion or something like that. Then I drop what I'm doing and concentrate on the poem and then I go back. But it's so unpredictable.

Sometimes I find that I'm able to write poetry in the morning and a little prose in the afternoon. It's almost never poetry and fiction; it's almost always poetry and nonfiction—an article perhaps. But every once in a while you're able to do it. I don't recommend it. There's something schizophrenic about that process. I think it's more important for a poet to learn to write prose, readable, sensible, logical prose than it is for a fiction writer to learn to write poetry. Sooner or later a poet—this is just the uses of the profession—sooner or later a poet's going to have to lecture or write an essay or introduce a volume by somebody else. These tasks come up, the journeyman work that is needed.

And there are certain poets who never learn to write a decent paragraph of prose, and so it's a limitation. It would be very interesting if we had any good prose by Robert Lowell but we don't. We just have little sketches. He was unable to write, say, a nice logical article about somebody he admired, like William Carlos Williams. His article on William Carlos Williams is dumb. Wallace Stevens, who thought very strongly about poetry and felt very strongly about it, writes the most illogical essays in the world. They make no sense. They're wonderful from sentence to sentence, but the paragraphs don't make any sense. So one should learn to write logically. I must say, in regard to Stevens, that the material that he wrote for his insurance work doesn't make any sense either. I read a talk about insurance that is included in his *Opus Posthumous.* It made no sense whatsoever. It was nice and empty.

Is there a poetic form you find easiest? Or one that's very difficult?

I find a lot of them very difficult; I don't find any of them easy. There are certain forms I find impossible. I've never been able to write a decent sonnet. Well, I wrote one decent sonnet but it didn't get any better than decent. And sapphics I've never been able to handle. I've tried sapphics a hundred times but I've not been able to make them go at all. On the other hand, some forms I prefer. I enjoy writing blank verse a great deal. It's not easy but it seems natural to me. And I like shorter rhymed poems for purposes of humor. They're not easy but I enjoy very much filing and polishing those little poems.

Each poem in Midquest *is a different form. Was it very difficult to switch from form to form to form like that? How did that idea arise?*

The idea arose simply because I got interested in the material and thought I needed to link the material, which is kind of semi-autobiographical, with a larger tradition, and I didn't know how else to do it. I didn't want to link it with the earlier formal tradition in poetry, James Russell Lowell and that sort of thing. I thought I wanted to link it with folk-like material, so I thought of samplers. I got out a book about samplers and looked at scores of samplers and learned a little bit about how women stitch things—not much, but enough to understand that there were different kinds of stitches. These objects were showpieces. And it occurred to me that it would be nice to have a kind of showpiece like an early American sampler of different kind of verse forms for stitches. And I made a list of different forms, everything from elegiacs to blank verse to free verse to whatever else is in the work, and I tried every one of them on my list and wrote the ones I could write. If someone went through the first two volumes he would see that my first attempts at blank verse are really not blank verse. They're just kind of five-beat lines that approximate blank verse. But by the third and fourth volumes I was writing blank verse. I will cheerfully admit that I thought I was writing blank verse from the beginning. But I wasn't. It's not easy to do.

In 1986 you wrote that one form you had not attempted was the epic poem. Do you think you ever will?

Oh, no, not in that sense. I am hoping to try a long comic poem in the burlesque epic mode, rather like *Don Juan,* but I have no ambitions to write a serious epic anymore. One time I projected one on George Washington, but that was beyond my reach, to tell the truth.

How did the structure of Midquest *come about? Did you come up with the idea for the four volumes as one book in the beginning, or did it grow out of writing some of the poems?*

It grew out of writing one poem, the first poem in the first book. I wrote it just as a poem, and later on in that half-sleep, half-waking stage before you get out of bed in the morning I realized that there was a great deal in there that I could explore. It was a kind of overture. And as soon as I thought of that word in my mind—overture or prelude, I'm not quite sure which—as soon as I thought of the musical analogy, then the whole structure came to mind. Four huge movements, as in a symphony, with themes and subthemes, in fugato organization and so forth. I don't mean this to be musically strict; it was just a loose analogy. I'm not trying to imitate symphonic form closely. It was just a way to organize a great deal of material and have it make sense.

Your book Castle Tzingal *is also a book of poems that tells a story. With your books of poetry, do you more often come up with ideas for the book or are you collecting separate poems?*

Very often I come up with the idea for the book after I've written a couple of poems and realized that there is a thread, a similarity, between them. Then I have formed an idea for a book, and I write to the organization of the book. *Castle Tzingal* tells a single story; it's almost like a little novella. In my mind it was a chamber opera, with all the separate poems being arias sung by the different characters. And that notion helped me organize it. But even books that look less organized, like *Source,* have thematic organizations. *Source* is organized around the idea of folk myth and folk motifs, the origins of narrative. *First and Last Words,* which is made up of prologues and epilogues, has an obvious organization. And I have a new book of poems coming out, a collection of epigrams; that's pretty obvious too.

What's that book called?

C. Roman numeral 100.

Are there a hundred epigrams?

That's right.

I'm interested in your writing routine. Do you write every day?

I try to write every day I can. Some days I'm on the road, some days there are things I have to do; we all have family business to take care of. We've got to water our chickens and milk the kangaroos. So these chores make it impossible some days. Some days—no longer—I had hangovers that prevented me from seeing the page, much less writing on it. But I have cut down on drinking. And then sometimes I'm just trifling and won't do it; I'd rather read a friend's book or answer some mail. But that's not often. You have to keep writing or you don't have any writing.

How do you feel when you've just completed a major project—a book of poetry or a novel. Do you take time off?

Usually I don't take much time off at that point because when you go down the home stretch on a largish project you've had to let everything else around you slide for a while. So there's a period of having to catch up on articles you promised, on letters you need to answer, on all kinds of business like that.

And it's really hard to do at that point, partly because you want to celebrate, partly because you want to commit suicide. Any writer, almost any writer I ever heard of, would tell you that it's a very depressing time right after you've finished a large project. You'll feel better later on, but . . . I guess it's the same as what they call a post-partum depression, but I don't mean it to sound like I've had a baby. I don't think there's much relationship between a woman having a baby and a woman writing a novel. Those are different experiences. But what you know is that part of your life is over and you're never going to get that period of time back; you're never going to feel those same ways again. Because the next project you work on will make you feel different.

Do you get the experience back to an extent when you read your work? Do *you go back and read your own work?*

Oh, I have to. I go on the road and read it to people, and also I have to edit it, I have to proofread it when it goes into anthologies. But just for the fun of it go back and pick up a book? I'd rather shoot my toes off. Past work is dead. It has no life in it for me. One exception. The first novel I wrote, *It Is Time, Lord,* I have always hated. And I had to read through it when they put out an anthology called *The Fred Chappell Reader.* And I thought, Oh, God, I can't stand it. But it seemed to have some stirrings of life. It's real dumb, but it seemed to have some stirrings of energy in it. And it may be that if enough time has elapsed that such personal feelings are not involved, a book could still have some interest for you. That one's twenty-five years old. But generally they look to me flat and mechanical. Because what I remember is not so much the surge of emotion I felt when writing, but working out the technical problems of writing.

You've written about the connection between poetry and farming; certainly your own writing has been informed by your rural childhood. Do you think farms—or cities—are more likely to breed poets than suburbs?

I think it has to do with the person, with the personality. I used to think the old classical saw, "Poets are born, not made," was kind of silly, and I still think it's fairly silly, but I do think after long regretful experience that some people are just never going to hear poetry, they're just never going to get it, just the same way some people can't hear music or can't taste different kinds of food. If you enjoy reading books of poetry, whether you're in the city or you're in the country or you're in the suburbs, then you have a fair chance of writing poetry.

Do you think that much good poetry could be written about the suburbs?

The great age of American suburban poetry was the 1950s. If you read people like Richard Wilbur and Howard Nemerov and Randall Jarrell, you're reading suburban poetry. Some of it's very good, as Wilbur and Nemerov and Jarrell are; some of it's kind of dumb. I guess I won't mention dumb names. But nevertheless, that's the period. They're also beginning about that time to write novels about suburbia, John O'Hara's novels. And George P. Elliot wrote *Parktilden Village,* Louis Simpson wrote *Riverside Drive.* Louis Simpson is a good suburban poet. So is Stanley Kunitz, for that matter. He is very good, maybe the best suburban poet.

What kind of time lag is there for you between experiencing something and writing about it? A few years ago you said that perhaps in twenty years you'd be writing poems about Greensboro.

Well, I have been writing poems about Greensboro; I just haven't been telling anybody around here that they're about Greensboro, because I don't want to disturb people or get into personal situations. But I haven't written many narrative poems about Greensboro, just lyrics and some character studies, that sort of thing. So the time lag is variable. Sometimes it's a few days, but more likely it takes a gestation that will be, well, from five up to thirty years. Carl Sandburg, when he worked at the newspaper and wrote poems, was always being teased by his colleagues because he would find a poem twenty years old at the bottom of his drawer and begin working on it just as if he'd put it down yesterday.

You've translated a lot of poetry. What languages have you translated?

Well, let's see, I've translated or adapted from Latin, French, Italian, and German. I don't really know German, and I don't know Italian very well, but I know enough to know the feeling I want to get from it. I have adapted some Greek but I used a pony and just plowed, went through the Greek words to make sure. But I don't think that counts.

What's the difference between translating and adapting?

Translating you aim for, as much as you can, the same words and the same language experience as you find in the other tongue. In adaptation you aim for an equivalence, something that's perhaps brought up to date, changed in its details so that it will have something like the original impact for a modern reader. In one of the forms you try to reclaim the experience; in the other you try to re-experience it.

Have you ever translated from English into another language?

I've translated some English into French. I used to do it as an exercise walking to school, in the back of my head. I've translated a few lines of Wordsworth. And sometimes when I used to drink beer out at a bar called The Pickwick, people would bug me with their poems. They'd want to talk about them and I didn't want to talk about them, so I'd say, This should be in French, and I'd translate it to French for them and say, This is not quite right, you need to work on your accent.

What is your favorite poem that you've written?

It's not a particularly good poem, but in my first book of poetry there's a poem called "Heath, Two Years Old." It reminds me of a period of our life, what our young lad was like then. And I like my love poems, of course, for the same sentimental reasons. But I don't think I've got any of my poems in memory, except maybe a poem called "The Story" because I've done it so many times at readings. I know lots of other people's poems; I used to know lots more than I do now. But mine don't interest me enough to memorize, to tell the truth.

Do you have a favorite poem, period?

The *Iliad,* I think.

What are you reading these days?

Well, I regularly review poetry books for the *Georgia Review,* so you can imagine. And I've always reviewed, for the last ten years, fiction and poetry for the Raleigh newspaper, so that's a lot of work. What am I reading for pleasure right now? A book called *The Mountains Won't Remember Us,* by Robert Morgan, a wonderful book of short stories, just terrific.

While talking about Castle Tzingal *once, you made reference to allegory in that work. Do you search for allegory in a work or does that just happen?*

Usually if you have to search then it's going to be a mechanical and clanky kind of allegory. You should probably—one should never make up prescriptions like this—but it's probably better for a writer to be working on a narrative and suddenly realize that it has allegorical potential, that without changing it, without violating the narrative, a little slant here or a little touch there will make it capable of allegorical interpretation. We're talking contemporary writing now. Dante didn't do it that way. He was right not to. But then, Dante could think in four categories at one time, and I can't do that.

In "The Homunculus," in Castle Tzingal, *there's a line, "All knowledge becomes of use." I wonder if that might be a motto for writers.*

Yes, I think so. You know, it's curious that you picked out that line because when I wrote it I was thinking specifically of someone I knew. A wonderful poet in the MFA program here named Amon Liner, who was about the brightest person I ever met in my life. And a friend of his, William Trotter, the historian and novelist, and I were talking about Amon once after his death, and Bill said, "Everything went into the hopper. Everything he was able to use." I thought about the little spy in the court of the ugly people, and I thought, that's a good characterization. . . . It was sad to lose Amon at such a young age.

Any thoughts on publishing with small presses vs. major houses?

No, I enjoy both. You probably don't want to publish a novel that has a chance to be popular with a small publishing house.

But you did that with I Am One of You Forever.

I did, because they published my poems, and I knew they weren't making any money on them, and I appreciated the loyalty that L.S.U. Press gave me. I did that as a goodwill gesture, a kind of thank-you note. But that's not a very canny move to do that. If you get a chance to go with a major publisher, you should. If a poet gets a chance to go with Viking Press, terrific, do so. But on the other hand, don't overlook opportunities. If you have a chance to publish with a small press, leap at it. You'll have a credit, in the first place; you'll have a book out. Maybe you'll get a job, who knows? Maybe you'll get a review somewhere. Take every opportunity you can, but, on the other hand, cover your ass too. Don't let people take advantage of you. They don't usually try to do that with poets because there's no point in it. They're not going to get anything if they did. But protect yourself. Do the best you can. It's very difficult for poets right now. That's one of the things the economic depression has made harder for the poet, a way to start. So take every opportunity you can. Don't be deeply discouraged; you're going to be discouraged a little bit every day, but don't be manic. And have fun. It's not worth doing if it's not a great deal of fun. If you don't have a sense of love and joy poetry would be a turgid existence. I know some poets for whom writing poetry became a burden, and I always felt very, very sad about that.

The Memorial Poem: A Fable

John Everhart lost his wife to a traffic accident. The couple had been married for twenty-six years and now John was so shattered and lonely that the remainder of his life appeared to him a desert of cinders. Though childless and without close relationship to their kin, John and Christine had been happy together, quiet and contented. They were not always happy every day and every moment; such an existence is not marriage, perhaps not even human. But for the most part they were possessed of a happiness as rare to see in our time as the pine siskin and the painted bunting.

For many months John was unmanned. Such sorrow and confusion were in him that he could barely manage to feed and bathe and clothe himself. There was no one he could look to for comfort or support. It was a wonder that the man survived this torn time with his faculties intact.

Six months after Christine's death John vowed to establish some suitable memorial to his wife. Now there was only the tombstone with her name and the implacable numbers and the weekly tribute of flowers he laid there. On every side of Christine lay silent strangers. The place of her grave began to seem inexpressive to John and his helplessness was a salt bitterness.

He was not a rich man, nor was he an artist of any sort. He was an assistant manager at a local supermarket, ill equipped to sculpt stone or compose hymns—and he had no money to pay for such things. But as soon as he thought of a memorial,

---

From *Small Farm* no. 6 (Fall 1977).

some measure of relief came into his thoughts, and he knew that his idea was a proper one.

In thinking about the possibilities of a memorial, he came at last to the notion of composing a poem. The construction materials of a poem are beautifully inexpensive. Poems are made of nothing but air, of nothing but words to be spoken in some sort of prearranged order, and words are available equally to the poor man and the rich. But poems can endure for a very long time, outlasting bronze and marble. There are poems written in tongues that the world has forgotten how to read, so that in one sense there are poems that have outlasted even themselves.

But just as he was no artist, neither was John a literary man. He was not even much of a reader, satisfying his desultory curiosity about the world with the newspaper and the television set. In high school a teacher had required him to read some poems, but he retained no impression of them.

Nevertheless, he determined to pursue his decision and to overcome the difficulties. Unable to find any poetry volumes in the local bookstore, he visited the public library and procured half a dozen books. He brought home Tennyson and Herrick and Dryden and three contemporary poets. But when he read through them all, John was plunged into a gloomy puzzlement tinged with dull anger. He could not say why his reading experience had been so depressing, but he felt the weight of it.

He had not expected to understand immediately what the poems said. Nor had he thought to learn to write poetry merely by reading a book; he understood the practice of poetry to be difficult. But he had not imagined the experience would be so utterly alien; he had not expected that poetry would wear such an uncaring face, that the lines would be so closely intent upon their own concerns that they would not bother to invite John Everhart as a reader.

Disheartened, he returned the books to the library.

But then one night he had a dream. In this dream a word appeared to him, and the word was in the form of a man clothed in a suit of red flame and wearing a black broad-brimmed hat. The word's presence was immense, overbearing, but John could not read the word. He knew only that it contained something of extreme importance for him. He strained to understand.

He woke, mumbling and trembling, seized with a hot thirst. Otherwise, though, he felt lightened and purified, as if a fever had broken.

He returned to the library and withdrew an anthology containing poems from different countries and centuries. These verses he found impenetrable for the most part, but he read the headnotes avidly, learning some facts and opinions. Then he read biographies of Victor Hugo and Heinrich Heine and Lord Byron. He began to lounge, as it were, about the outskirts of poetry, picking up information and gossip, wondering about the sad or sordid shapes of poets' lives, wondering about them as personalities. He was rather like a teenager intrigued by movie stars.

He began to dream at night of an undiscovered race of people dwelling in the caverns of Tibet.

Then one day while he was going over an inventory sheet, a line of poetry by Sir Thomas Wyatt came into his head and grasped his mind with such force and clarity that he dropped his pencil. He felt something akin to an electric shock; his eyes widened and his mouth flew open. What had struck him so hard was the direct simplicity of the statement and the simplicity of the words. He drummed his finger on his clipboard in time to the rhythm of the line. Perhaps this had been the obstacle from the beginning, he thought. He had strained too hard to understand; poetry was simpler than he had imagined. He tried to recall some other lines but could not.

When he got home that evening he took up eagerly the anthology of poetry, expecting to read through it as easily as the newspaper sports page. Alas. The poems still guarded their secrets.

But important things were beginning to take place in John Everhart's inner life.

Little by little, almost tediously, he was beginning to understand. He began, without noticing, to change some of his habits. Certain television programs he no longer watched; they now seemed bland and vapid. He had always taken an evening constitutional when the weather was fair, but now he walked far in every weather and these perambulations took on a graver tone day by day. He noticed more of his surroundings, not only birds and plants, but also details like the shapes of asphalt patchings in the streets, configurations of grain in sawn wood, reflections of streetlamps on wet leaves, echoes of his steps in midnight avenues.

He became moodier, gloomy sometimes, sometimes elated, but when he was content, his contentment was richer than before. His speech had got slightly disordered; he found himself repeating aloud words like *splay* or *emphatic* or *holm-oak.* He rescued a stray cat and named it Hodge. His pulse rate slackened and his breathing slowed, so that he felt a little like an athlete freshly in training. He started drinking wine with his evening meals and taking a cognac with his morning coffee. New lines of experience creased his face.

Poetry is a mode of consciousness; it affects not the mind only but the neural paths too and the blood chemistry. All these changes in John were subtle; he never noticed them.

Three years had passed since Christine died, but John had stopped counting the long days. He had at last gained enough confidence to attempt the study of poetry composition. He purchased a book that explained rhyme and meter and stanza forms and the rest of it. It was hard going, and he wondered what all this prattle of ingenuity had to do with poetry. Yet he kept on, laboring faithfully, though he felt he would never gain any competence in technique.

Still, it is possible to absorb technique without being fully aware of it, to become proficient by dint of experience rather than by intellection.

This casual process may have taken place in John Everhart, for in matters of technique it is impossible to realize just where and when and how one has grasped control of it. Those dozen or so poems that John had learned by heart now sounded different than they had earlier: the vowels were rounder and fuller, the consonants pricklier, the caesurae more profoundly silent.

And although he might deny the fact, a fair measure

of viable technique was now his and, as he continued his studies, the outlines of his memorial poem began to take shape.

It was four years after this, during his evening walk, that a vision of Christine, seven years dead, came to him. She appeared in the air as he stood on a corner not far from his home. In the vision Christine was dressed in a loose white linen dress with short flowing sleeves. Her hair was done up in antique fashion and bound with a fillet, and she wore sandals. She moved her arms and hands strangely before her, as if she might be playing a harp. Over and over she drifted her hands in the air. Her lips moved and, though the vision was silent, he made out the words:

John, my dear husband.

Then the vision went away like a mist dispersing.

He thought for a long time before he realized that his wife had appeared to him in the guise of Penelope. Penelope was the patient and faithful wife of Odysseus who for twenty years raveled in the dark what she wove by daylight. She who was history's sweetest figure of constancy and devotion had invested herself with the features and lineaments of John's own Christine.

As he thought these things, John experienced both joy and sadness. It was marvelous that she had shown herself in this most fitting image. Yet the lovely Penelope was now Greek dust for thirty centuries. Heartbreaking millenia stretched between them and John believed that it must be his study of poetry which had caused Christine to come to him in a form so distant and irrecoverable. She had become a kind of object—like a painting or a statue; she was more clearly defined but less personal than when his sorrow had been as fresh and keen as broken glass.

The vision gave John to understand what he had gained and lost; whether the loss or the gain were greater he could not tell. Without the intense personal and immediate qualities of his sorrow he was lonelier than ever, and yet he had fixed Christine in a steady shape that he could return to at will and with some ease of mind.

At this point he began work on his memorial, writing actual words on paper.

The history of the poem itself is a history apart from its inception. The poem might be matter for scholars and textbooks, but the way in which it speaks to readers, the way in which it touches those attuned to its particular moods and changes, is determined by the difficult process of its birth. Pure literary merit is not always the best gauge of the true worth of a poem, and this memorial that keeps warm and alive and sad the love of a man for his mate has virtues that might go unremarked.

Let them go, then, unremarked. It is in the unremarkable, in the ordinary tragic designs of our lives, that our best triumphs are achieved. It is only the ordinary that is the least bit extraordinary.

UNDER DISCUSSION
Donald Hall, General Editor

Volumes in the Under Discussion series collect reviews and essays about individual poets. The series is concerned with contemporary American and English poets about whom the consensus has not yet been formed and the final vote has not been taken. Titles in the series include:

Elizabeth Bishop and Her Art
edited by Lloyd Schwartz and Sybil P. Estess

Richard Wilbur's Creation
edited and with an Introduction by Wendy Salinger

Reading Adrienne Rich
edited by Jane Roberta Cooper

On the Poetry of Allen Ginsberg
edited by Lewis Hyde

Robert Bly: When Sleepers Awake
edited by Joyce Peseroff

Robert Creeley's Life and Work
edited by John Wilson

On the Poetry of Galway Kinnell
edited by Howard Nelson

On Louis Simpson
edited by Hank Lazer

Anne Sexton
edited by Steven E. Colburn

James Wright
edited by Peter Stitt and Frank Graziano

Frank O'Hara
edited by Jim Elledge

On the Poetry of Philip Levine
edited by Christopher Buckley

The Poetry of W. D. Snodgrass
edited by Stephen Haven

Denise Levertov
edited by Albert Gelpi

Forthcoming volumes will examine the work of William Stafford and Gwendolyn Brooks, among others.

Please write for further information on available editions and current prices.

Ann Arbor ***The University of Michigan Press***